BEYOND THE BEYOND

UNAUTHORIZED GAME SECRETS

PRIMA PUBLISHING
Rocklin, California
(916) 632-4400

NOW AVAILABLE FROM PRIMA

Computer Game Books

1942: The Pacific Air War–The Official Strategy Guide
The 11th Hour: The Official Strategy Guide
The 7th Guest: The Official Strategy Guide
Across the Rhine: The Official Strategy Guide
Alone in the Dark 3: The Official Strategy Guide
Angel Devoid: The Official Strategy Guide
Armored Fist: The Official Strategy Guide
Ascendancy: The Official Strategy Guide
Buried in Time: The Journeyman Project 2–The Official Strategy Guide
CD-ROM Games Secrets, Volume 1
CD-ROM Unauthorized Game Secrets, Volume 2
CD-ROM Classics
Caesar II: The Official Strategy Guide
Celtic Tales: Balor of the Evil Eye–The Official Strategy Guide
Civilization II The Official Strategy Guide
Command and Conquer Secrets and Solutions
Cyberia: The Official Strategy Guide
Cyberia^2 Resurrection: The Official Strategy Guide
Dark Seed II: The Official Strategy Guide
Descent: The Official Strategy Guide
Descent II: The Official Strategy Guide
DOOM Battlebook
DOOM II: The Official Strategy Guide
Dragon Lore: The Official Strategy Guide
Dungeon Master II: The Legend of Skullkeep–The Official Strategy Guide
Fleet Defender: The Official Strategy Guide
Frankenstein: Through the Eyes of the Monster–The Official Strategy Guide
Front Page Sports Football Pro '95: The Official Playbook
Fury^3: The Official Strategy Guide
Hell: A Cyberpunk Thriller–The Official Strategy Guide
Heretic: The Official Strategy Guide
I Have No Mouth and I Must Scream: The Official Strategy Guide
In The 1st Degree: The Official Strategy Guide
Kingdom: The Far Reaches–The Official Strategy Guide
King's Quest VII: The Unauthorized Strategy Guide
The Legend of Kyrandia: The Official Strategy Guide
Lords of Midnight: The Official Strategy Guide
Machiavelli the Prince: Official Secrets & Solutions
Marathon: The Official Strategy Guide
Master of Orion: The Official Strategy Guide
Master of Magic: The Official Strategy Guide
Mech Warrior 2: The Official Strategy Guide
Mech Warrior 2 Expansion Pack Secrets and Solutions
Microsoft Arcade: The Official Strategy Guide
Microsoft Flight Simulator 5.1: The Official Strategy Guide
Microsoft Golf: The Official Strategy Guide
Microsoft Space Simulator: The Official Strategy Guide
Might and Magic Compendium:
   The Authorized Strategy Guide for Games I, II, III, and IV
Mission Critical: The Official Strategy Guide
Myst: The Official Strategy Guide, Revised Edition
Online Games: In-Depth Strategies and Secrets
Oregon Trail II: The Official Strategy Guide
Panzer General: The Official Strategy Guide
Perfect General II: The Official Strategy Guide
Power Pete: Official Secrets and Solutions
Prima's Playstation Game Secrets: The Unauthorized Strategy Guide
Prince of Persia: The Official Strategy Guide
Prisoner of Ice: The Official Strategy Guide
The Residents: Bad Day on the Midway–The Official Strategy Guide

Return to Zork Adventurer's Guide
Ripper: The Official Strategy Guide
Romance of the Three Kingdoms IV: Wall of Fire–The Official Strategy Guide
Shannara: The Official Strategy Guide
Sid Meier's Civilization, or Rome on 640K a Day
Sid Meier's Civilization II: The Official Strategy Guide
Sid Meier's Colonization: The Official Strategy Guide
SimCity 2000: Power, Politics, and Planning
SimEarth: The Official Strategy Guide
SimFarm Almanac: The Official Guide to SimFarm
SimIsle: The Official Strategy Guide
SimLife: The Official Strategy Guide
SimTower: The Official Strategy Guide
Stonekeep: The Official Strategy Guide
SubWar 2050: The Official Strategy Guide
Thunderscape: The Official Strategy Guide
TIE Fighter Collector's CD-ROM: The Official Strategy Guide
Under a Killing Moon: The Official Strategy Guide
WarCraft: Orcs & Humans Official Secrets & Solutions
WarCraft II: Tides of Darkness–The Official Strategy Guide
Warlords II Deluxe: The Official Strategy Guide
Werewolf Vs. Commanche: The Official Strategy Guide
Wing Commander I, II, and III: The Ultimate Strategy Guide
X-COM Terror From The Deep: The Official Strategy Guide
X-COM UFO Defense: The Official Strategy Guide
X-Wing Collector's CD-ROM: The Official Strategy Guide

Video Game Books

3DO Game Guide
Battle Arena Toshinden Game Secrets: The Unauthorized Edition
Behind the Scenes at Sega: The Making of a Video Game
Breath of Fire Authorized Game Secrets
Breath of Fire II Authorized Game Secrets
Complete Final Fantasy III Forbidden Game Secrets
Donkey Kong Country Game Secrets: The Unauthorized Edition
Donkey Kong Country 2–Diddy's Kong Quest Unauthorized Game Secrets
EA SPORTS Official Power Play Guide
Earthworm Jim Official Game Secrets
Earthworm Jim 2 Official Game Secrets
GEX: The Official Power Play Guide
King's Field Game Secrets Unauthorized
Killer Instinct Game Secrets: The Unauthorized Edition
Killer Instinct 2 Unauthorized Arcade Secrets
Mortal Kombat II Official Power Play Guide
Mortal Kombat 3 Official Arcade Secrets
Mortal Kombat 3 Official Power Play Guide
Ogre Battle: The March of the Black Queen–The Official Power Play Guide
PlayStation Game Secrets: The Unauthorized Edition, Vol. 1
Secret of Evermore: Authorized Power Play Guide
Secret of Mana Official Game Secrets
Sega Saturn Unauthorized Game Secrets
Street Fighter Alpha–Warriors' Dreams Unauthorized Game Secrets
Ultimate Mortal Kombat 3 Official Arcade Secrets
Urban Strike Official Power Play Guide, with Desert Strike & Jungle Strike

HOW TO ORDER:

For information on quantity discounts contact the publisher: Prima Publishing, P.O. Box 1260BK, Rocklin, CA 95677-1260; (916) 632-4400. On your letterhead include information concerning the intended use of the books and the number of books you wish to purchase. For individual orders, turn to the back of the book for more information.

Visit us online at http://www.primapublishing.com

BEYOND THE BEYOND™

UNAUTHORIZED GAME SECRETS

BY
ANTHONY
JAMES

Acknowledgments

Anthony James and Jesus Running-Bear wish to thank: Italian Princess, Rogue, QV-Fresh, Eyegore, &TKD-P

Dedicated to: Dorian, Jose, Lily, and Nataly

Project Editor: Julie Asbury

Illustrator: Caylon Balmain

This fully independent edition is a product of Prima Publishing and is not affiliated with Sony Computer Entertainment. Beyond the Beyond ™ and its characters are trademarks of Sony Computer Entertainment.

Important:

ISBN: 7615-0865-1

Library of Congress Catalog Card Number: 96-69509

Printed in the United States of America

96 97 98 99 GG 10 9 8 7 6 5 4 3 2

CONTENTS

CHAPTER ONE

✥ INTRODUCTION

In its first year of existence, the PlayStation® has enjoyed remarkable success in all genres, but one: role-playing games. However, this should all change with Beyond the Beyond, the first great role-playing game for the system. Highlights of the game include a long, involved story line with many secrets, puzzles, and battles. The "exploration" view is a traditional, two-dimensional, over-the-head view, but the battle scenes feature an intricate and appealing three-dimensional approach. With hundreds of enemies and items to encounter in a huge world, this title is sure to provide many hours of entertainment.

This book has been designed to help you in your quest. Each adventure is broken down to highlight your objectives, foes, and goods, and each chapter includes a basic walkthrough. You'll learn the best techniques, the locations of secret items, and strategies for success. For your reference, an index has been provided with a brief summary of each enemy and item. As *Beyond the Beyond* is a non-linear title, some of the steps in your quest can be performed at different times than those recorded here. This book simply highlights the most effective way through the game. *Beyond the Beyond* is one of the toughest, most frustrating games you'll probably ever face, so try to relax and have fun. After all, it's only a game!

THE STORY LINE

Long ago, a great war raged between the Beings of Light and the Warlocks of the Underworld. Death and destruction were rampant, and the Earth itself came perilously close to annihilation. Realizing what had almost occurred, the two sides agreed to a truce in which the Beings of Light would rule above the surface, while the Warlocks would command everything below. The Kingdom of Quamdar was set as a boundary between the two. Peace reigned for many years, but as of late, unusual events have begun to take place, including the appearance of an ominous cloud over Quamdar.

You play as Finn, a child of destiny who must lead a hearty band of adventurers against an ancient evil and restore order to the land. A long, difficult journey awaits. So heed the call, and begin your adventure.

CHAPTER TWO

✤ GAME BASICS

Basic controls for the playstation are as follows:

D-PAD - ↑ ↓ ← →

L1 OR R1 - TALK/SEARCH

△ - TALK/SEARCH

X - CALL UP MENU/CONFIRM A SELECTION

O - CANCEL MENU OR SELECTION

STATUS MENU

The following is a key for each characteristic on your Status Menu:

Class - Character's profession
Condition - Displays any illness or abnormality
VP - Vitality points
LP - Life points
MP - Magic points
Attack - Attack strength with weapons
Defense - Defense strength with armor/shields
Speed - Speed with armor/weapons equipped
EXP - Current experience accumulated
Next - Experience needed to advance a level
Strength, defense, speed, IQ, and luck are the natural abilities of each character.

FIGHTING

It goes without saying that combat is an important element of any role-playing game. When attacked, your characters will appear in three-dimensional view with all participants displayed on the battle-field. Your characters will stand in a formation of

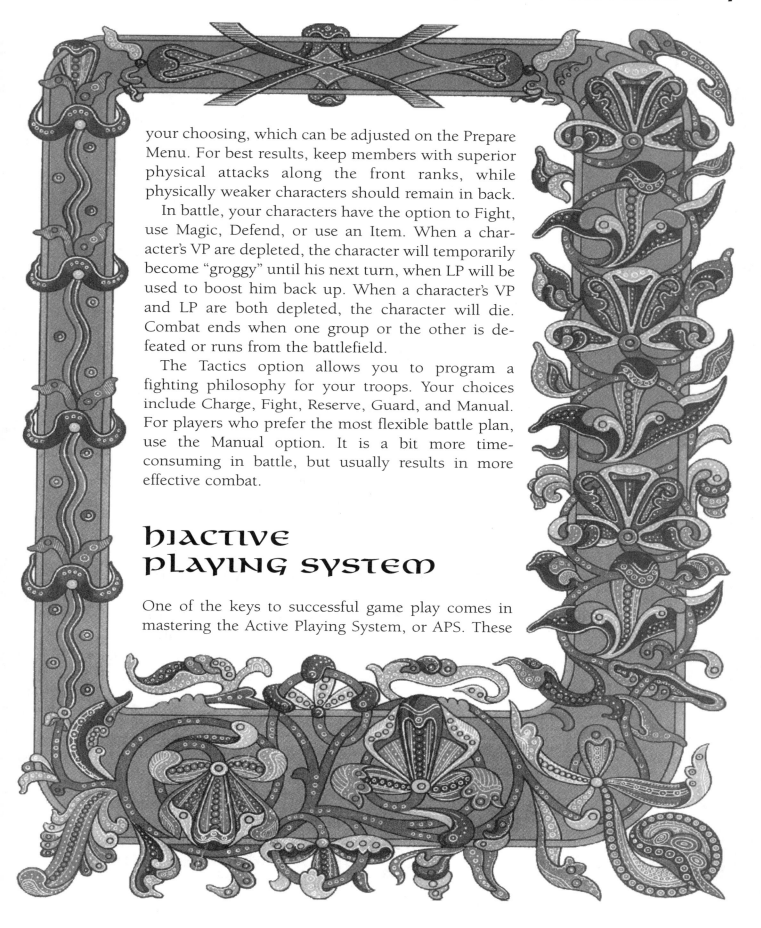

your choosing, which can be adjusted on the Prepare Menu. For best results, keep members with superior physical attacks along the front ranks, while physically weaker characters should remain in back.

In battle, your characters have the option to Fight, use Magic, Defend, or use an Item. When a character's VP are depleted, the character will temporarily become "groggy" until his next turn, when LP will be used to boost him back up. When a character's VP and LP are both depleted, the character will die. Combat ends when one group or the other is defeated or runs from the battlefield.

The Tactics option allows you to program a fighting philosophy for your troops. Your choices include Charge, Fight, Reserve, Guard, and Manual. For players who prefer the most flexible battle plan, use the Manual option. It is a bit more time-consuming in battle, but usually results in more effective combat.

Hiactive Playing System

One of the keys to successful game play comes in mastering the Active Playing System, or APS. These

are special maneuvers that can be performed in battle to enhance your battle skills. By learning to utilize the APS, you'll increase your chances of performing a Gold or Blue Attack. As one of your characters begins a physical attack, you'll notice a colored diamond over that character. When the blue diamond appears, rapidly press the X and ↓ on the controller to attempt a Blue Attack, which includes Double Attacks. When the gold diamond appears, rapidly press the X and ↑ on the controller to attempt a Gold Attack. These attacks often prove the difference in a tough battle.

EXPLORING THE LAND

Upon leaving a city, you'll find yourself on the Map Screen. Here, you'll travel over a variety of terrains and meet a host of dangerous creatures. Try not to stay on the open road too long, or you may pay the ultimate price.

ABNORMAL CONDITIONS

In battle, your party may be exposed to any of the following afflictions: Sleep, Confusion, Impaired

Sight, Silence, Poison, Paralysis, Curse, or Turn to Stone. These conditions will adversely affect your combat capabilities, and in some cases may lead to death if left untreated. Most can be remedied by Magic or Items, while others can only be cured by the Church.

TOWN FACILITIES

Inns Buildings labeled "Inns" can be used to recover lost VP, LP, and MP. A night's stay will replenish each character to maximum level. The cost to stay varies from town to town.

Supply Shops Buildings with a bottle symbol are the best places to purchase supplies such as Herbs, Antidotes, Jewels, Potions, etc.

Weapons/Armor Stores Buildings with sword or shield symbols carry a variety of weapons and armor. The selection varies in each city, and gets better the farther you progress.

Churches These are generally long, rectangular buildings with altars inside. In any Church you can save a game, cure a condition, or resurrect a dead ally.

SAVING YOUR GAME

Beyond the Beyond is a long game. Be sure to take the time save your adventure at every possible point. Believe me, there's nothing worse than making great progress through the game, dying, and being knocked back to a distant save point. Saved games can be recorded at any Church.

GENERAL HINTS

Monster attacks are determined by the distance your party travels, not the time your party spends traveling. Backtracking greatly increases your chances of being attacked, so don't do it!

When you are traveling, always carry as many Healing Herbs and Antidotes as you can. You never know when you will encounter a new monster.

Build your characters' levels! When your characters increase in level, they gain more Vitality Points, Strength, Magic...Everything. There is no shame in hanging out in front of a town and slaughtering monsters for personal advancement.

Utilize the Storage Trunk in the basement of Annie's house. Throughout the game, you will pick up Items that are necessary for the completion of the game. You cannot sell or discard them. After you use the Item to its extent, it just takes up valuable space in your character's inventory. You can use that space for Healing Potions.

If you enter a town, search EVERYTHING!!! Chests, vases, cupboards, trees, bushes, drawers... EVERYTHING.

While you are in a town, talk to everyone. The townspeople (as lame as they may seem) will provide important information regarding your quest.

In combat, when your character flashes, or when the enemy flashes, rapidly tap the X on the controller. Tapping the X increases your character's chances for a Critical Hit, a Counterattack, a Double Attack, or a successful Retreat. The X can turn the tide of any battle.

If you encounter a monster that you have never seen before, destroy it as fast as you can. There is a good chance that it will be tougher than anything you have faced before. Use the Monster Compendium (Appendix)! It will give you an idea of what to expect from the bad guys.

In all towns, the most expensive Items are the best! Basically, you get what you pay for.

Do not equip Items that are called "Dark," "Death," or "Chaos." These will curse your party member until a priest can remove the curse.

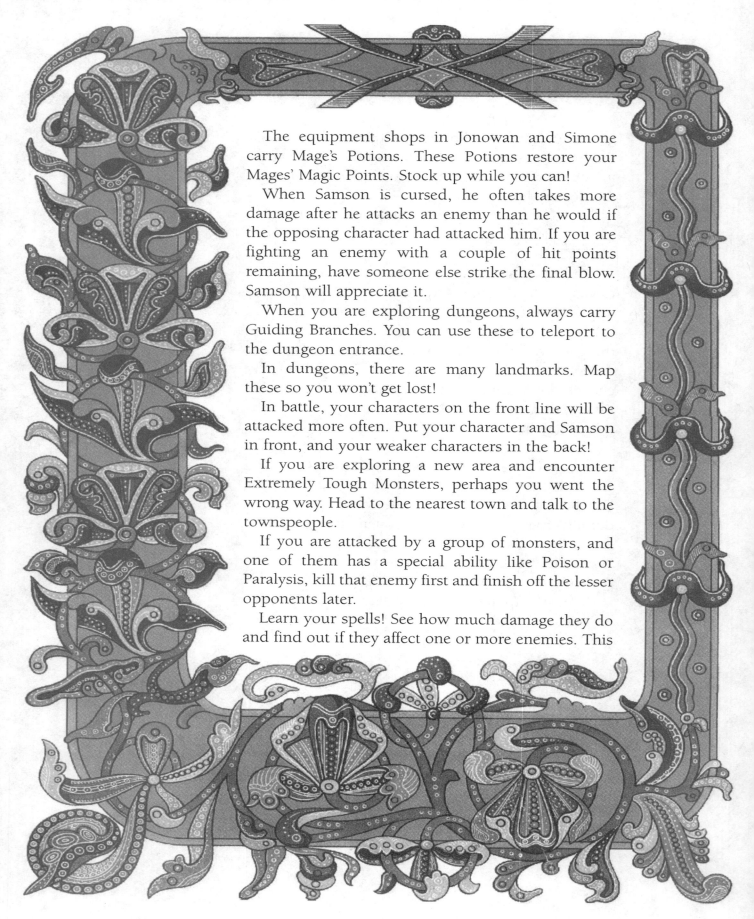

The equipment shops in Jonowan and Simone carry Mage's Potions. These Potions restore your Mages' Magic Points. Stock up while you can!

When Samson is cursed, he often takes more damage after he attacks an enemy than he would if the opposing character had attacked him. If you are fighting an enemy with a couple of hit points remaining, have someone else strike the final blow. Samson will appreciate it.

When you are exploring dungeons, always carry Guiding Branches. You can use these to teleport to the dungeon entrance.

In dungeons, there are many landmarks. Map these so you won't get lost!

In battle, your characters on the front line will be attacked more often. Put your character and Samson in front, and your weaker characters in the back!

If you are exploring a new area and encounter Extremely Tough Monsters, perhaps you went the wrong way. Head to the nearest town and talk to the townspeople.

If you are attacked by a group of monsters, and one of them has a special ability like Poison or Paralysis, kill that enemy first and finish off the lesser opponents later.

Learn your spells! See how much damage they do and find out if they affect one or more enemies. This information will prove invaluable in the heat of battle.

BOSS STRATEGIES

When you encounter a Boss in any adventure game, there are specific strategies you can use to overcome him. Before you actually fight the Boss:

✤ **Put your best armored fighters on the front line and your least armored comrades in the back.**

✤ **Don't give your most offense-oriented character a ton of Potions. Instead, give the Healing/Magic Potions to the weaker members. That way, while your heavy hitters are at work, your other guys can heal everyone.**

✤ **Have an aggressive attitude. With each round comes more damage to your party. The faster you defeat any enemy, the less rounds he will spend attacking your group.**

✤ **When you fight the last Boss, you have a choice as to who you will bring against him. Use strategy. Do you want a strong offense?**

Defense? Non-Magic Attacks? Bring the characters that are best suited for your strategy. Don't forget to build their levels!

Use the first round to prepare:

❖ **Cast Attack Spells and use Items to increase your party's defenses.**
❖ **Heal wounded members.**
❖ **Take Mage's potions to increase your Magic Points.**

During Combat:

❖ **Experiment. Try different powerful Spells and see which ones do the most damage. When you find the most devastating, abuse it!**
❖ **Take note of the order in which the characters attack. Does the Boss always attack first? If any of your characters can move before the Boss, give them some Healing Potions so they can heal their friends before the Boss immediately kills them. Example: If your character always goes first, Edward has 10 Vitality Points remaining, and the Boss always uses a Spell**

that damages everyone by 20 Vitality Points, your character can heal Edward to 30 or 40 Vitality Points so he can survive the Boss's initial attack!

❖ Keep your characters alive as long as possible. The more characters that attack per round, the fewer rounds the battle will last.

❖ Capitalize on the Boss's strategic blunders! If the Boss has been hammering your party with powerful Spells, and he uses a much less effective Spell, use this break as an advantage. Assist the party members who need help, because the Boss will soon resume his Powerful Magic Attack strategy.

❖ Don't waste Annie's Magic Points on offensive Spells like Holy Light. Save her Magic for the Healing Rain.

❖ If at first you don't succeed, find out what went wrong. Did you have enough Healing Potions? Were there Items in your inventory that you could have used better? Did the guy with all of the Healing Potions die first? **LEARN FROM YOUR MISTAKES!**

❖ If you get completely wiped out, build up your levels and try again!

CHAPTER THREE

✦ CHARACTERS

The world of Beyond the Beyond contains a number of colorful characters. These are the characters who will round out your party:

Finn (your character): the main character. Finn is both a capable fighter and a spellcaster. During the course of the adventure, Finn will learn some revealing secrets about his heritage, and lead the fight to save the world. Finn begins as a swordsman and can be promoted to a hero.

STEINER This baby dragon is a trusted ally of Finn. When used in combination, the two can deliver a nasty dual attack! Later in the game, he'll mature into a full-fledged dragon and will prove to be a valuable resource.

ANNIE Annie is the daughter of Sir Galahad. As a Cleric, she possesses advanced healing abilities. She also has a huge crush on Finn and, as a result, will do anything to help his cause! She can be promoted to High Cleric.

PERCY Percy is Annie's brother and a brave warrior in his own right. To save the team, he'll make the ultimate sacrifice.

SIR SAMSON Samson is a powerful Soldier who serves as a bodyguard to Prince Edward. Early in the game, he'll be hampered by a sorceress's curse, but once he's freed, stay out of his way. His hand-to-hand fighting skills are second to none! Upon promotion, he'll become a Gladiator.

EDWARD Edward is the Prince of Marion. Although his fighting skills are suspect, his magical abilities are strong. Use these abilities to overcome the toughest enemies. Edward begins as a Magician and can eventually become a Mage.

TONT Tont is a lost soul, whom you may find during your first visit to Simone. Despite his unusual appearance, Tont is courageous and effective in the art of magic. Continue to develop his powers, and you'll have an extremely valuable ally. Tont will start the game as a Conjurer, before being upgraded to a Summoner.

DOMINO Domino is a Pirate who'll cross paths with you at different times during the adventure. When he joins the party, you'll add a strong fighter with some spellcasting talent. Later on, he'll be able to rise to the rank of Captain.

LORELE In Barbaros, the warrior princess Lorele will become an ally when you rescue her. As a Monk, she'll bring a strong combination of fighting and healing abilities on her mission of vengeance. As she gains experience, she'll develop into a Master Monk.

NOTE: You'll only be allowed a maximum of five characters at any one time.

CHAPTER FOUR

✣ MAGIC

One of the most important elements of any good role-playing game is magic, and beyond the beyond is no exception. Throughout the game, you will acquire powerful spells for your characters, and you'll need every one of them to survive. Following are descriptions of each spell available to your characters.

FINN

Escape Similar to a Guiding Branch, this will return the party to an entrance of a cave, maze, or level.

Fire Projects a ball of flames at enemies. (Levels one and four work against a single opponent; levels two and three work against multiple opponents.)

Heal Restores Vitality Points to one ally. (Level one has a maximum of 13 VP, level two: 20 VP, and level three: 30 VP.)

Illusion Reduces the perception of an opponent. (Level one affects a single opponent; level two affects multiple opponents.)

Mystery A spell with random results that can hurt or help your enemy.

Steiner Steiner breathes flames onto multiple enemies.

Thunder Delivers a bolt of electrical damage. (Levels one and four work against a single opponent; levels two and three work against multiple opponents.)

ANNIE

Awaken Restores a sleeping ally. (Level one affects one ally; level two affects all allies.)

Cure Serves as an antidote to an unnatural condition.

Heal Restores Vitality Points to one ally. (Level one has a maximum of 13 VP, level two: 20 VP, and level three: 30 VP.)

Heal Rain Restores Vitality Points to all allies.

Holy Light Projects a beam of pure energy. (Level one affects one enemy; level two affects all enemies.)

Silence Neutralizes the magical powers of an enemy. (Level one affects one enemy; level two affects all enemies.)

Steal Drains the Magic Points from an enemy.

PRINCE EDWARD

Attack Enhances the fighting prowess of an ally. (Level one affects one ally; level two affects all allies.)

Confusion Reduces the perception of an opponent. (Level one affects a single opponent; level two affects multiple opponents.)

Fire Projects a ball of flames at enemies. (Levels one and four work against a single opponent; levels two and three work against multiple opponents.)

Ice Projects a ball of ice at enemies. (Levels one and four work against a single opponent; levels two and three work against multiple opponents.)

Silence Neutralizes the magical powers of an enemy. (Level one affects one enemy; level two affects all enemies.)

Thunder Delivers a bolt of electrical damage. (Levels one and four work against a single opponent; levels two and three work against multiple opponents.)

Void Sucks an enemy into a mystic dimension. (Level one affects one enemy; level two affects all enemies.)

TONT

Attack Enhances the fighting prowess of an ally. (Level one affects one ally; level two affects all allies.)

Firedrake Summons a Fire Demon to attack all enemies.

Steal Drains the Magic Points from an enemy.

Summon Summons a random monster to attack. (Level one affects one enemy; level two affects all enemies.)

Titan Summons an Earth Demon to attack all enemies.

Tolle Summons a Wind Demon to attack all enemies.

Undhine Summons a Giant Troll to attack all enemies.

DOMINO

Awaken Restores a sleeping ally. (Level one affects one ally; level two affects all allies.)

Confusion Reduces the perception of an opponent. (Level one affects a single opponent; level two affects multiple opponents.)

Illusion Reduces the perception of an opponent. (Level one affects one enemy; level two affects all enemies.)

Slow Drains the speed of an enemy. (Level one affects one enemy; level two affects all enemies.)

Wind Projects a blast of powerful air. (Level one affects one enemy; level two affects all enemies.)

LORELE

Cure Serves as an antidote to an unnatural condition.

Defense Enhances the defensive prowess of an ally. (Level one affects one ally; level two affects all allies.)

Heal Restores Vitality Points to one ally. (Level one has a maximum of 13 VP, level two: 20 VP, and level three: 30 VP.)

Heal Rain Restores Vitality Points to all allies.

Holy Light Projects a beam of pure energy. (Level one affects one enemy; level two affects all enemies.)

Sleep Renders an enemy unconscious. (Level one affects one enemy; level two affects all enemies.)

Wind Projects a blast of powerful air. (Level one affects one enemy; level two affects all enemies.)

chapter five
✥ level walkthroughs

village of isla 1

This is your chance to get acquainted with the characters and controls, and begin your adventure.

THE FOES

None.

THE GOODS

- ✤ **Short Sword**
- ✤ **Antidote**
- ✤ **Herb**
- ✤ **Storage Trunk**
- ✤ **Light Shield**
- ✤ **Flask**

WALKTHROUGH

The story begins as you return from a hard day of training with your father, Sir Kevins. You awake in the house of your mentor, Galahad, and find your trusty dragon, Steiner, waiting faithfully. At this point, you will take control of your character for the first time. Search the barrels to collect some basic goodies, and then head out to find Galahad.

Galahad asks you to go to the Cave of Spirits to collect some Spirit Water as a favor. He gives you a

Flask to hold the water. The only clue he provides is to take the right path when you reach the fork in the road, because the left is more dangerous. As a reward, he'll take you to Marion Castle if you're successful. Before heading out, go to the basement to find a Short Sword, Antidote, Herb, and Light Shield. You'll also find a Storage Trunk that can be used to store excess inventory. When you're ready, venture out into the village.

In the village, take the time to become familiar with the town. For insurance, you may want to purchase some extra Herbs from the merchant (three to four should be plenty). Then stop by the church to save your game. Exit the village at the southern opening. The Cave of Spirits lies southeast of the village.

CAVE OF SPIRITS

OBJECTIVES

To honor the request of Galahad, you must enter the Cave of Spirits and fill your Flask with Spirit Water. Along the way, you must also save Annie from a deadly swamp beast.

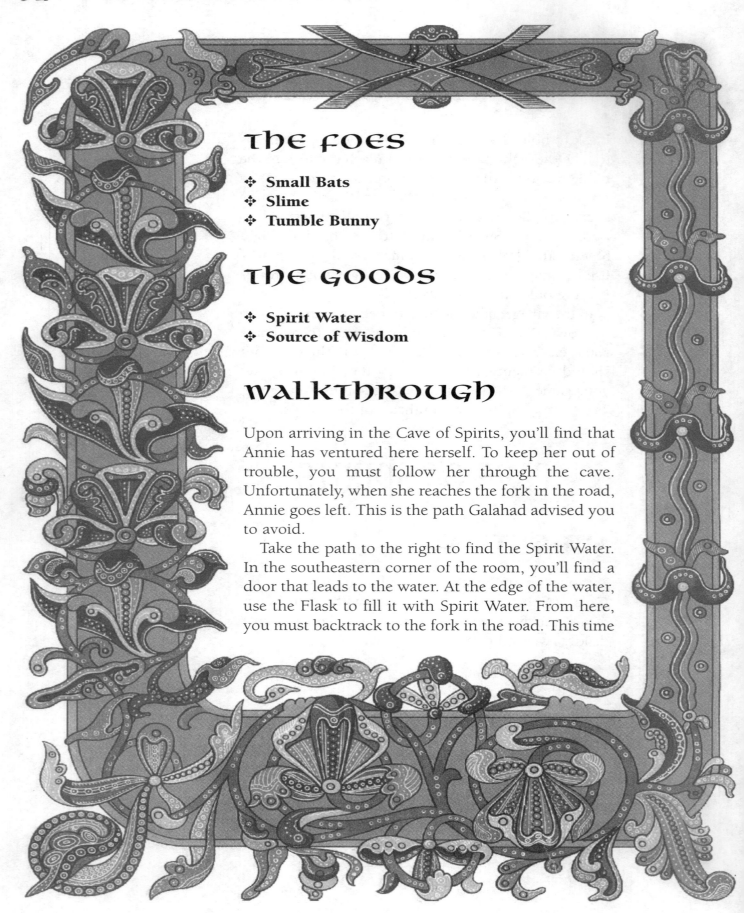

THE FOES

❖ **Small Bats**
❖ **Slime**
❖ **Tumble Bunny**

THE GOODS

❖ **Spirit Water**
❖ **Source of Wisdom**

WALKTHROUGH

Upon arriving in the Cave of Spirits, you'll find that Annie has ventured here herself. To keep her out of trouble, you must follow her through the cave. Unfortunately, when she reaches the fork in the road, Annie goes left. This is the path Galahad advised you to avoid.

Take the path to the right to find the Spirit Water. In the southeastern corner of the room, you'll find a door that leads to the water. At the edge of the water, use the Flask to fill it with Spirit Water. From here, you must backtrack to the fork in the road. This time

take the left path to find Annie. Northwest of the entrance, you'll find a treasure chest with a Source of Wisdom. Continue through two more rooms to reach Annie. The Kraken will pull her into the swamp. To save her, use the Flask and pour Spirit Water into the swamp. The Kraken will release her, and she will join the party. Now return the Spirit Water to Galahad.

As you return to Isla, Annie's brother, Percy, returns to the village with a message. It seems as if the Kingdom of Marion is under attack from the evil forces of Bandore. With a new goal defined, Percy joins your team. Your next stop is Marion Kingdom.

Before leaving the village, be sure to save your game and load up on supplies. When you're ready, exit the town at the northern gate and head north to Marion.

MARION KINGDOM

OBJECTIVES

Marion Kingdom has been overrun by the troops of Bandore. You must find Sir Samson and help him to rescue Prince Edward.

THE FOES

- ❖ Bats
- ❖ Bandore Troops

THE GOODS

- ❖ Ring of Defense
- ❖ Smoke Bomb
- ❖ Prison Key
- ❖ Royal Pendant

WALKTHROUGH

Upon walking into town, you'll find a sign that reads, "Sir Samson, Prince Edward will be executed unless you surrender." Take the time to look around. In the graveyard, search behind the northwest tombstone, and you'll find the Ring of Defense. Next, head north to see Marion Castle. You won't be able to get in yet, but if you search the northern section of the flower bed to the west of the castle, you'll find a treasure chest with a Smoke Bomb.

After you take the time to investigate the town and talk to the inhabitants, a mini-sequence will begin

that features Samson fighting off the Bandore Troops and disappearing into the cemetery. To find Samson, enter the house to the west of the graveyard and search under the desk. You'll find a door to a hidden room in the basement. In the hidden room, hit the wall switch. This will open a secret tunnel in the graveyard.

Enter the tunnel for a shortcut into Marion Castle. You'll have to face some enemies, but nothing too stiff, yet. When you reach the path blocked by rocks, the team will unite to clear the road. In the next section of the tunnel, you'll find Samson. If you agree to help rescue Prince Edward, he will join your party.

At the end of the tunnel, climb the stairs and you'll find yourself within the dungeon of Marion Castle. In the first few cells you pass, you'll find some of Marion's captured troops. At the last cell in the dungeon, Prince Edward waits to be rescued, but his cell is locked. Enter the room to the immediate west of the cell. After you defeat the Bandore Troops, you'll collect the Prison Key. Use the Prison Key to free Prince Edward. Samson suggests the party travel to Zalagoon, and Edward joins the group.

To exit the castle, head back toward the tunnel. Here, you'll run into the first of the emperor's heavy hitters, Ramue. In a brief confrontation, she curses Samson, which results in him dropping back to level

one status. Strangely enough, she lets you go. For now, that is.

In the tunnel, Samson suggests that the group split into two. Along with Edward, he will meet the team at the Border Church to the east. Edward gives you the Royal Pendant to show to the church pastor. After taking the escape tunnel, you'll appear on the outskirts of the city. Take this opportunity to reenter the city, buy supplies, save your adventure, and rest at the inn for 50 Gold Pieces. When you're prepared, head east for the Border Church.

BORDER CHURCH

OBJECTIVES

You're on the road to Zalagoon, but to get there you must cross the border. At the Border Church, solve the puzzle of Venus and make your way through the secret passage through the border.

THE FOES

- ❖ **Killer Bee**
- ❖ **Zombie**
- ❖ **Bat**
- ❖ **Goblin**
- ❖ **Giant Scorpion**
- ❖ **Poisonous Frog**
- ❖ **Green Slime**
- ❖ **Mold**
- ❖ **Kobold Lord**

THE GOODS

- ❖ **Resist Jewel**
- ❖ **Antidote**
- ❖ **Blizzard Card**
- ❖ **Counter Orb**

WALKTHROUGH

After escaping the forces of Bandore in Marion, head east to the Border Church. You'll find it nestled in the southern base of the mountains. Before entering the

church, explore the forest on the eastern edge of the building. You'll find a treasure chest with a Resist Jewel. Now, enter the church and search the eastern barrels to find a handy Antidote.

The pastor will be friendly, but until you show him the Royal Pendant, he won't be very helpful. Use the Royal Pendant, and the door behind the pastor will open. If you wait at the end of the hall, you'll rendezvous with Samson and Edward. Because the border is guarded by troops, you must solve a riddle to open a secret passage through the mountain.

The riddle states, "You must crown Venus's brow with a laurel and tierra. When she smiles upon the world, you shall be one step closer to Arawn." The answer to the riddle lies in rearranging the eight tiles in such a way that the face makes sense. When the eight tiles are in place, the ninth will rise up in the center, and the door to the secret passage will open. If you try to leave before completing the puzzle, you'll have to face Ramue and her forces, which at this point will be an almost impossible task.

Before you enter the passage, be sure to take advantage of the pastor's offer to save a game. In the temple, take the opening in the floor. At the bottom of the stairs, search the middle vase to find the Blizzard Card. At the closed gate, press the lever to

the left to open the passage. At this point, Percy will sacrifice himself to allow you to escape.

In the tunnels, you may come across Brother Thomas, who will ask you to guide him out. If you help him, he will help you later on down the line. When you reach the light, you'll be at the end of the tunnel.

Outside the tunnel lies the Mountain Cottage, an inn where you can rest and recover for a nominal fee. At the bar, look for Brother Thomas, who will make himself available for any services you may require.

To the north of the cottage, you'll see a cave opening. You don't need to enter it yet, but if you need some experience, take a chance. You may even see the Sleeping Dragon, who will block your path as you try to explore deeper sections of the cave.

To the east of the cottage, you'll find a tree with an opening in the base. The goal here is to work your way up the levels of the tree. If you fall in a hole, you'll drop down a level, so use the brown acorns to cover the openings. If you back the acorn into a wall, though, you'll be unable to push it farther and will have to reset the puzzle, so strategically think about how you must move each one to the corresponding hole. Sometimes the best path might not be the shortest, most obvious one. When you reach the top of the tree, you must climb along the vine to another tree. At the next tree, you must work your way down each level by dropping through the openings in the floor. Sometimes you may land on a cobweb, which will bounce you back up, so keep plugging away. Eventually, you'll reach the ground floor. Then head northeast to Zalagoon.

ZALAGOON

OBJECTIVES

With Marion under Bandore's control, you must attempt to persuade the king of Zalagoon for help against the evil forces.

THE FOES

- ✢ **Orks**
- ✢ **Spinning Tail**
- ✢ **Kobold Lord**
- ✢ **Thief**
- ✢ **Flying Mouse**

THE GOODS

❖ **Magic Bean**
❖ **Bronze Key**

WALKTHROUGH

The general mood in Zalagoon is not very good. It seems that Advisor Glade has made some extremely unpopular decisions, and the people are convinced that Bandore will next turn its attention to Zalagoon. Because of the low morale and suspicious climate, the townspeople will not help you until you have talked to someone at Zalagoon Castle. You can stay at the inn for 100 Gold Pieces.

Head north and go to the castle gate to see the king. At the gate, your credentials will be questioned. The advisor will say that you must wait in town to prove your identity. On the path back, a young boy will tell you of a secret entrance into the castle through the underground waterways.

Arriving back in town, you will now be able to buy supplies from the local merchants. Take the time to upgrade your weapons and armor, and then search any of the town's three wells. This will allow you to drop down and explore the lower region of the city.

To start, search the southernmost well, just west of the inn. In the sewers, you'll find a number of pathways that lead to dead ends. You'll also notice that if you drop down into different sections of the water, the current will drag you in different directions. From the starting point, take the first two eastern bridges, and then head west over another bridge. When you reach the wall, walk north until you see a water passage with a half-circle opening in the wall and enter. Travel to the southwest corner of the sewer until you find a ladder that leads into the cellar of the tavern. You'll find a treasure chest with the Bronze Key. With the Bronze Key in hand, walk back to the half-circle opening and continue to the northeast corner of the level until you reach the locked door. Use the Bronze Key and follow the sewers north, then west at the opening in the wall until you find a small room with crates and barrels. Take the ladder up, and you'll find yourself in a side section of the castle.

Here, you will meet Sir Bison. He'll offer his help, and tell you to return to town and meet the advisor's men. So now you must head back through the sewers into town.

In town, you'll be invited to the castle. Walk through the gate and into the courtyard to have an audience with the king and queen. With Edward an Samson's credentials still in doubt, Samson will be asked to

prove his identity with a challenge of strength. Unfortunately, because of the curse, he will fail, and the king will refuse to accept your claims. Thus, he will not support Marion against Bandore. Leave the castle and return through the sewers to confer with Bison. He will suggest that a trip to Simone, in the Southwestern Mountains, may be useful in helping Samson to break free of Ramue's curse. The queen will give a Magic Bean to Edward. Legends say that it must be used to restore the peace to Marion, so keep it safe. Bison instructs you to return to town when the curse has been broken. Now you must head back through the sewers yet again, and back into town. Purchase some supplies, and then save your game.

At this point, exit the town and head south along the eastern edge of the country to find Ophera.

OphERA

OBJECTIVES

Ophera is a small town where you can rest and reload for the battles ahead.

THE FOES

None

THE GOODS

✣ **Flame Card**
✣ **Smoke Bomb**

WALKTHROUGH

Ophera is a small town you'll stumble across on your trip to Simone. Just southeast of the Desert Ruins, along the coastline, you'll find the city.

In town, you'll find that many people are talking about the tower that has appeared over the Desert Ruins. One man suggests that it may be the Tower of Arawn, a symbol of the coming evil.

In the small house to the right of the church, search the vase to find a Flame Card. In the second house to the right of the church, search the vase to find a Smoke Bomb.

There's really not a lot to do here, so stock up on weapons and supplies, rest at the inn for 40 Gold Pieces, and head south to Luna.

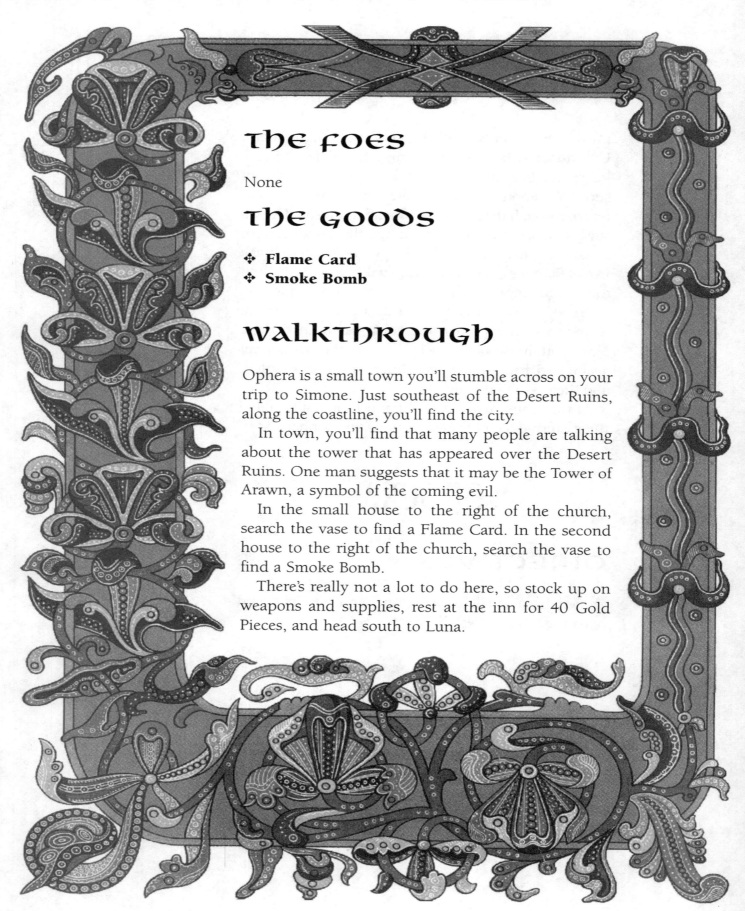

LUNA

OBJECTIVES

Like Ophera, there won't be any real purpose to Luna yet, other than to stock up your inventory and advance the story line. You will gain some tantalizing hints about important items you'll need later in the game.

THE FOES

None.

THE GOODS

None.

WALKTHROUGH

Luna is a port town. Around town, you'll notice a lot of treasure chests that will be unreachable for the

time being. Nothing much will happen on your first trip here, but you'll hear many stories of the wild nightlife. You'll also hear about the Moon Crescent. Now what could that be?

At the store, you'll overhear an argument between a merchant and his employee, who has been cheated out of a valuable treasure called the Vase of Life.

Stay at the inn for 120 Gold pieces, and when you've prepared to venture out, head north to reach the Mist Caves, which lead to Simone.

MIST CAVES

OBJECTIVES

To reach Simone, you must successfully tread through the maze of the Mist Caves.

THE FOES

❖ **Roper**
❖ **Lizard Man**

- ❖ Ghost
- ❖ Elf
- ❖ Amazon Priestess
- ❖ Blood Pudding
- ❖ Wizard
- ❖ Dark Priest
- ❖ Ghoul

THE GOODS

- ❖ Broad Sword
- ❖ Flame Card
- ❖ Power Gauntlet
- ❖ Magic Emerald

WALKTHROUGH

From Luna, walk north along the coastline until you reach the foot of the mountains. Here, you'll find the entrance to the Mist Caves.

Upon entering the cave, pass through the door to reach the next level. From here, take the southeastern door to find a treasure chest with a Broad Sword. Next, take the northeastern door and continue through the hole in the wall. Enter the

southwestern wall and take the stairs next to the door. From here, climb the vine to the left and continue north. Climb the stairs, head east, and then continue south. At the two doors, enter the western door and climb the two vines along the ledge until you reach the Magic Emerald. Collect the emerald and return down the first vine. Enter the cave and head north until you reach the stairs. Head south for the two doors, and take the eastern one this time. Climb the vine and enter the cave to find a Flame Card. Take the stairs to the east and then head north to the next set of stairs. On this level, take the vine to the upper platform to find a Power Gauntlet. From here, continue south through the middle path. Outside, climb the vine to reach the final group of caves. Inside, head northeast to reach the exit to the next level, and once there, head north to the next exit. Head north once more, and in the next room head east to exit. The final door will be in the southern area of the room.

When you find yourself back on the Map Screen, head southeast of the cave exit, and you'll find Simone.

SIMONE

OBJECTIVES

You enter Simone in hopes of breaking the curse that has been placed on Samson.

THE FOES

None

THE GOODS

- **Source of Agility**
- **Antidote**
- **Tempest Jewel**

WALKTHROUGH

After a tough passage through the Mist Caves, pay 40 Gold Pieces to stay at the inn.

Around town, you'll notice a woman who is searching for her missing son, Tont. It's rumored that he disappeared with a Magic Cape that has made him invisible. At the house south of the church, search the boiling pot of food. You'll find a Source of Agility.

Apparently, the town's most powerful magic user, Master Zeon, is training to protect the world from disaster at the Mystic Shrine and cannot be bothered. He's even blocked the eastern road with a magic boulder to prevent anyone from interrupting him.

Take the western path to reach a house with an old man mixing a strange brew. Give him the Magic Emerald, and his recipe will explode. When you awake, you'll see a strange yellow blob. It won't have much to say if you talk to it, but you'll notice that it will follow you around. Trust me, this is a good thing.

Back in the main section of town, head up the northern path to the Mystic Tree. In the tree, you'll find a collection of magic users studying. They seem to be most worried about the temple of Arawn.

In the Mystic Tree, search the vases to find an Antidote and the treasure chest to find a Tempest Jewel. Don't worry about the room with the locked door, as you can't get in there now. If you're interested in some background about the Temple of Arawn, scour the bookshelves for some helpful

information. Four levels down, you'll enter a room with elaborate decorations and a huge purple rug. Talk with the high shaman of Simone, and he'll try, unsuccessfully, to break the curse on Samson. It seems as if only Zeon has the power, and of course he's unavailable. Return to town and stock up for your return through the Mist Caves. Your next destination is Ophera, where you will prepare for a visit to the Desert Ruins.

When you leave town, the yellow blob will transform into the missing young boy, Tont. Apparently, if a bad dose of Transformation Powder has altered his appearance, but he is eager to be a part of the team. He will join your party in its quest, and become a powerful ally.

Desert Ruins

OBJECTIVES

In the depths of the Desert Ruins lies the Moon Crescent. Find it and you'll be able to partake in the nightlife of Luna.

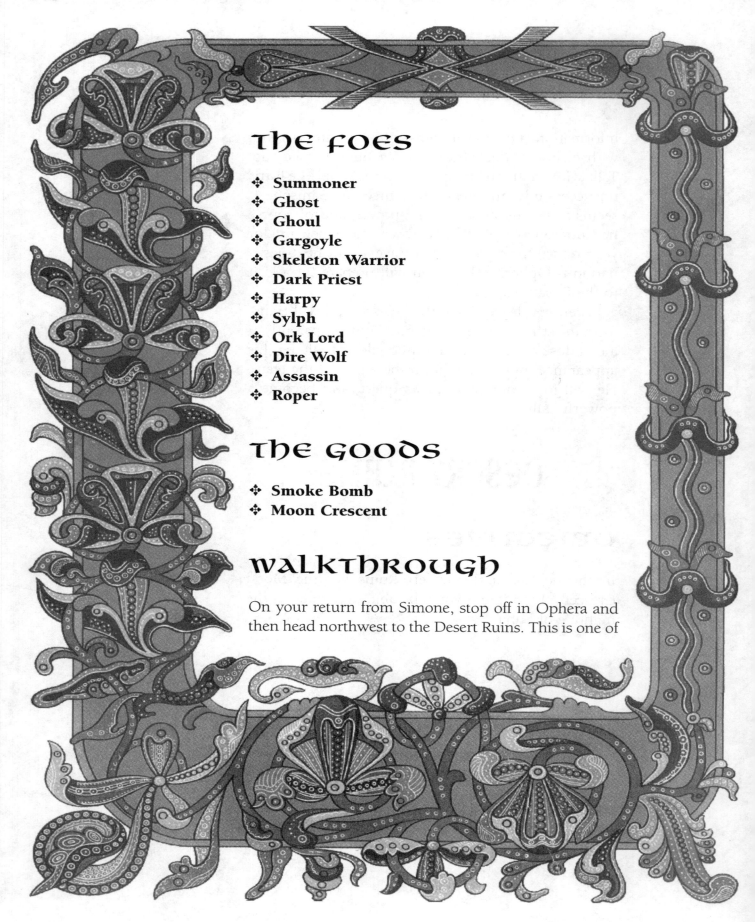

THE FOES

- ✣ **Summoner**
- ✣ **Ghost**
- ✣ **Ghoul**
- ✣ **Gargoyle**
- ✣ **Skeleton Warrior**
- ✣ **Dark Priest**
- ✣ **Harpy**
- ✣ **Sylph**
- ✣ **Ork Lord**
- ✣ **Dire Wolf**
- ✣ **Assassin**
- ✣ **Roper**

THE GOODS

- ✣ **Smoke Bomb**
- ✣ **Moon Crescent**

WALKTHROUGH

On your return from Simone, stop off in Ophera and then head northwest to the Desert Ruins. This is one of

the longest and toughest mazes you'll face early in the game. The enemies are strong, so you might need to run a lot here. Be sure to buy a Guiding Branch before entering, as it will save you a lot of time and effort.

Upon entering the temple, take the first staircase to the east and climb the vine to enter into the depths of the ruins. In most levels of the ruins, there is no one best path to take. The key to making your way through each level is to understand that by stepping on a blue switch, you'll alter walkways to travel upon or through.

For the most part, the first five levels of the Desert Ruins are fairly routine. On level one, you'll start in the northwest corner and must make your way to the northeast corner to exit. On level two, walk along the eastern wall to the southeast portion of the level and continue slightly northwest. The exit is in the center of the room. On level three, you'll need to head northeast and then south to activate the switches and clear a walkway along the floor path. The exit can be found in the southwest corner. On level four, head northwest to the stairs leading down, and then continue southeast to the stairs leading up to an exit. On level five, venture to the northeast corner to move the switch path to the southern position, and then return to the southeast corner and wind through the floor path to an exit in the northwest corner.

Level six will be the trickiest you'll face. To start, walk south to the first switch and activate it so that the path is connected in the southern position. Then walk west. Continue until you reach a switch in the southeast portion of the maze. You'll find it just east of a staircase. Here, activate the switch so that the western path rests south of the stairs. Head for the eastern path of this switch and continue northeast until you reach the third switch of the level. Activate this switch so that the eastern path bisects the eastern wall and divides the two treasure chests. Now, head west along the western path of this switch, back to the first switch in the northwest. Activate this switch once again to move the eastern path north, and continue south along the western wall. At the staircase, walk down into the floor path and continue northeast to reach the treasure chest with the Moon Crescent.

When you have the Moon Crescent, use a Guiding Branch to exit the ruins and head back to Ophera.

LUNA II

OBJECTIVES

Return to Luna with the Moon Crescent, and you will gain valuable information about Domino, as well as access to a number of hidden treasures and valuable shop items.

THE FOES

None.

THE GOODS

- ❖ **Critical Jewel**
- ❖ **Source of Growth**
- ❖ **Healing Herb**

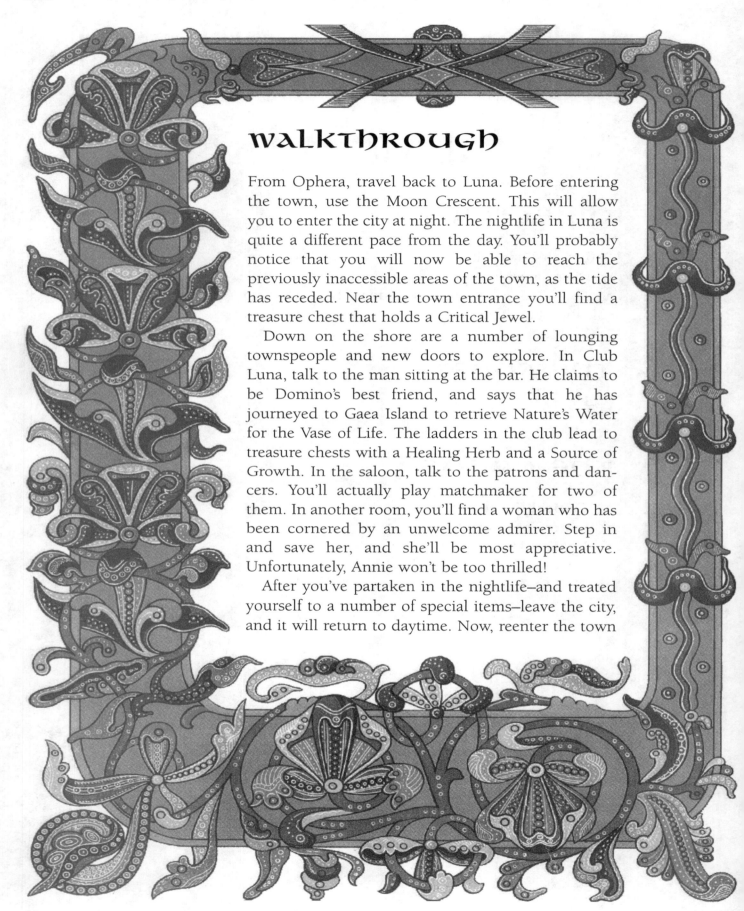

WALKTHROUGH

From Ophera, travel back to Luna. Before entering the town, use the Moon Crescent. This will allow you to enter the city at night. The nightlife in Luna is quite a different pace from the day. You'll probably notice that you will now be able to reach the previously inaccessible areas of the town, as the tide has receded. Near the town entrance you'll find a treasure chest that holds a Critical Jewel.

Down on the shore are a number of lounging townspeople and new doors to explore. In Club Luna, talk to the man sitting at the bar. He claims to be Domino's best friend, and says that he has journeyed to Gaea Island to retrieve Nature's Water for the Vase of Life. The ladders in the club lead to treasure chests with a Healing Herb and a Source of Growth. In the saloon, talk to the patrons and dancers. You'll actually play matchmaker for two of them. In another room, you'll find a woman who has been cornered by an unwelcome admirer. Step in and save her, and she'll be most appreciative. Unfortunately, Annie won't be too thrilled!

After you've partaken in the nightlife—and treated yourself to a number of special items—leave the city, and it will return to daytime. Now, reenter the town and head to the dock. You'll find a man sitting at a table who wants to trade the Moon Crescent for the Statue of Gaea. Because you'll need it soon, make the trade. Exit the town and head east to the Valley.

The valley

OBJECTIVES

To reach Jonowan Village, and ultimately Gaea Island, your party must travel through the Valley.

The foes

- ✤ **Sylph**
- ✤ **Skeleton Warrior**
- ✤ **Lizard Warrior**
- ✤ **Roper**
- ✤ **Gargoyle**
- ✤ **Bug Bear**
- ✤ **Ork Lord**
- ✤ **Dire Wolf**

THE GOODS

❖ **Angel Ribbon**

WALKTHROUGH

Just northeast of Luna, you'll find a crease through a pair of mountains. This is the road to Jonowan. Enter the Valley, and you'll find yourself in the midst of a thick fog. Be sure to grab the treasure chest near the opening to collect an Angel Ribbon.

As you make your way through, you'll notice strange white skulls that will pull you from point to point. The first few will be fairly routine. When you reach the area with four skulls, stand under the southern skull and walk east. Walk along the eastern wall and continue to make your way north until you reach a section of the Valley where the fog clears up.

In this section, you must travel on the path under the waterfall and find the vine northwest of the rainbow. Climb the vine and head east so that you will be grabbed by the next skull. To the north, you'll find the Valley exit. From here, continue southeast on the Map Screen to find Jonowan.

ONOWAN VILLAGE

OBJECTIVES

On the trail of Domino, you arrive in Jonowan to find more clues to his whereabouts.

THE FOES

None.

THE GOODS

❖ **Source of Wisdom**

WALKTHROUGH

After traversing through the Valley, rest at the inn for 50 Gold Pieces. Traveling through town, you'll find yourselves most unwelcome visitors. It seems that the townspeople have had their share of problems

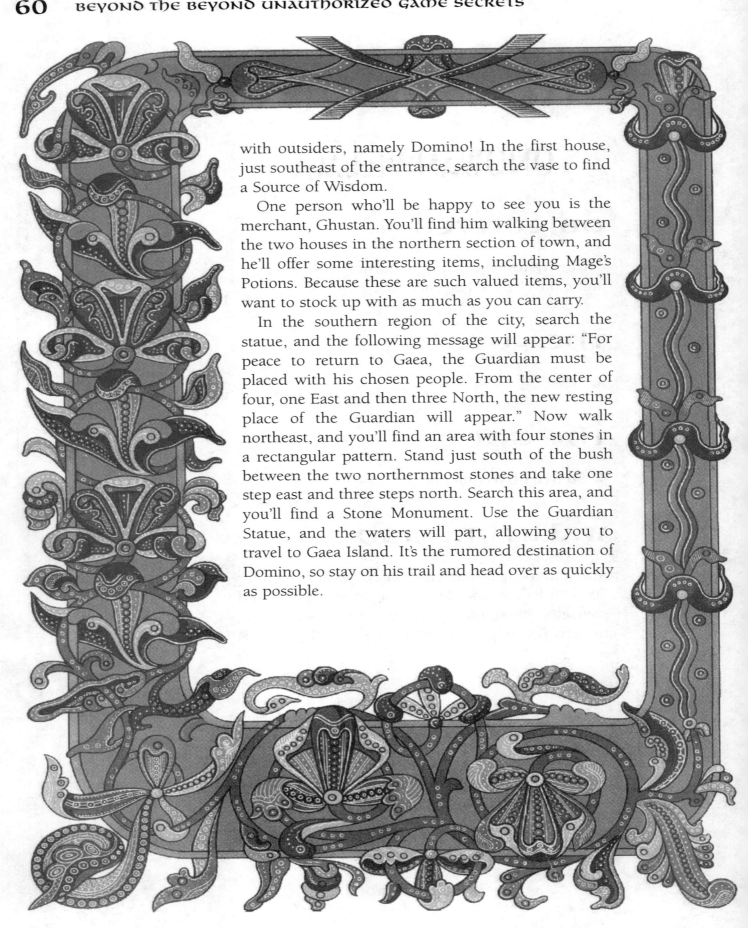

with outsiders, namely Domino! In the first house, just southeast of the entrance, search the vase to find a Source of Wisdom.

One person who'll be happy to see you is the merchant, Ghustan. You'll find him walking between the two houses in the northern section of town, and he'll offer some interesting items, including Mage's Potions. Because these are such valued items, you'll want to stock up with as much as you can carry.

In the southern region of the city, search the statue, and the following message will appear: "For peace to return to Gaea, the Guardian must be placed with his chosen people. From the center of four, one East and then three North, the new resting place of the Guardian will appear." Now walk northeast, and you'll find an area with four stones in a rectangular pattern. Stand just south of the bush between the two northernmost stones and take one step east and three steps north. Search this area, and you'll find a Stone Monument. Use the Guardian Statue, and the waters will part, allowing you to travel to Gaea Island. It's the rumored destination of Domino, so stay on his trail and head over as quickly as possible.

GAEA ISLAND

OBJECTIVES

Enter the temple to find Domino and the Vase of Life.

THE FOES

- ❖ **Naga**
- ❖ **Cockatrice**
- ❖ **High Elf**
- ❖ **Bug Bear**
- ❖ **Ice Warrior**
- ❖ **Gargoyle**
- ❖ **Water Leaper**
- ❖ **Imp**
- ❖ **Lizard Warrior**
- ❖ **Siren**
- ❖ **Harpy**
- ❖ **Living Armor**
- ❖ **Water Demon**

THE GOODS

- ❖ **Vase of Life**
- ❖ **Battle Dress**
- ❖ **Battle Axe**

WALKTHROUGH

As you cross the parted waters to Gaea Island, they will close behind you. Head north, up the peninsula, and into the temple. Upon entering the temple, search the stone, just south of the staircase. You'll find a Stone Monument, similar to the one in Jonowan. Use the Guardian Statue, and the waters will part once again. Now, take the stairs up to level two.

As you make your way up the levels, beware of two hazards. First, avoid the glowing purple disks on the ground. They will sap your Magic Points, which will be critical in the battle with the Water Demon. Second, avoid the holes in the floor, which will drop you down a level and force you to retrace your steps.

On level two the lights are off, but the exit is easily located in the northwestern corner. Just past the row of three Guardian Statues, you'll find the stairs.

On level three, you'll find yourself being shadowed by a walking Guardian Statue. To get it off your tail,

you must lead it to the spot with a Guardian symbol, which can be found along the southern edge of the level. From here, head east to the next staircase.

On level four, pass the Guardian Statues to the west, and one will follow you. You'll find its matching symbol to the north. To the west lies the exit.

On level five, the Guardian Statue will pick you up early, so just head south to take care of it. To the east, you'll find a treasure chest with a Battle Axe. From here, the exit is to the west.

On level six, there are no statues to drag, so just head northeast to reach the stairs.

On level seven, there are two statues to take care of. Take the first one to a Guardian symbol directly south, but watch your step. There are a number of hazards along the way. From here, walk to the northwest corner of the room to find the exit. Another Guardian Statue will be waiting, and you can lead it to a symbol just west of the first statue's resting place. If you find the treasure chest, open it to collect a Battle Dress. When you're ready, exit the room.

On level eight, you'll find yourself in a small room. Use this break to heal and prepare for the battle in the northern chamber. If you have any Flame Cards, you may want to pass them to Samson. As for Mage's Potions, keep them in Annie's hands. To the north, you'll enter a room with a pool of water. Domino lies motion-

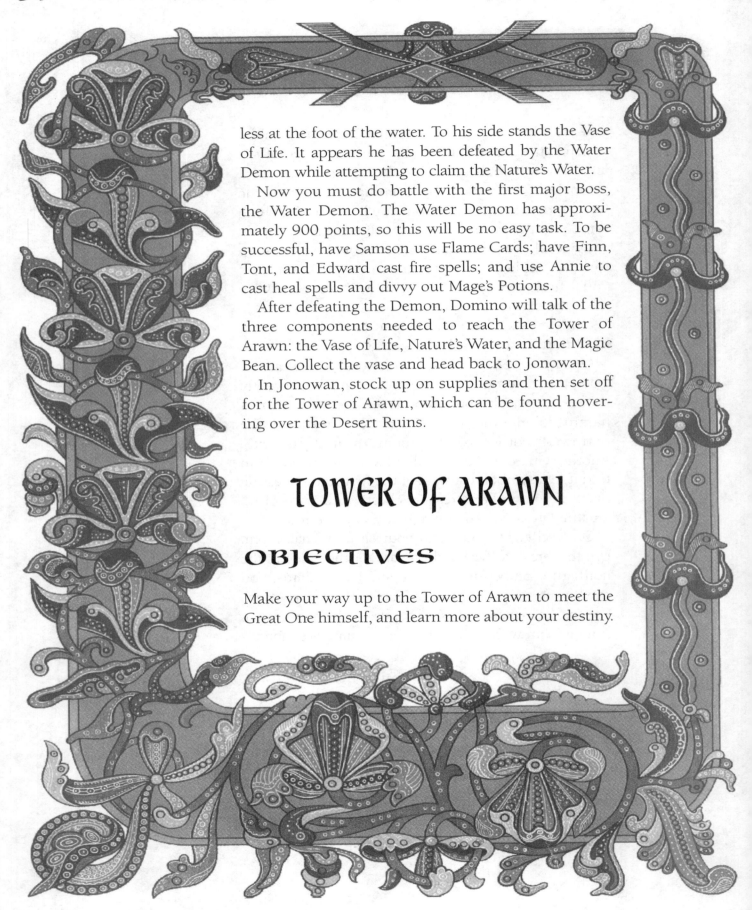

less at the foot of the water. To his side stands the Vase of Life. It appears he has been defeated by the Water Demon while attempting to claim the Nature's Water.

Now you must do battle with the first major Boss, the Water Demon. The Water Demon has approximately 900 points, so this will be no easy task. To be successful, have Samson use Flame Cards; have Finn, Tont, and Edward cast fire spells; and use Annie to cast heal spells and divvy out Mage's Potions.

After defeating the Demon, Domino will talk of the three components needed to reach the Tower of Arawn: the Vase of Life, Nature's Water, and the Magic Bean. Collect the vase and head back to Jonowan.

In Jonowan, stock up on supplies and then set off for the Tower of Arawn, which can be found hovering over the Desert Ruins.

TOWER OF ARAWN

OBJECTIVES

Make your way up to the Tower of Arawn to meet the Great One himself, and learn more about your destiny.

THE FOES

- **Mantrap**
- **Clay Golem**
- **Imp**
- **Raise**
- **Mystic Fungus**
- **High Elf**
- **Siren Harpy**
- **Illusionist**
- **Yeti**
- **Living Armor**
- **Naga**
- **High Ork**
- **Flying Mouse**
- **Water Leaper**

THE GOODS

- **Tempest Sword**
- **Hammer**
- **Ancient Tablet**
- **Light Orb**

WALKTHROUGH

Reenter the Desert Ruins and walk north through the middle door. Stand on the platform in the center of four gold platforms and use the Vase of Life and the Magic Bean. A huge vine will sprout up and serve as a ladder to ascend to Arawn's Tower. After the vine grows, take the first staircase to the east and then follow the long northern staircase to reach the vine and begin your climb up.

On each platform of leaves, you'll need to collect drops of dew. They look like light blue orbs. Search the water drop to collect it; then walk to a pink bud or small leaf and search again to grow a new path. The puzzle aspect of this lies in that you can only take ten steps with the water drops before you spill them, and must recollect the water.

The giant vine is fairly routine for the first few sections. The only real problem you may encounter will come on level seven. When you climb up from the southeastern vine, the vine in the north will look like an easy exit to reach. Unfortunately, the water drops east of the bud are too far away. To solve this puzzle, you must move in a counterclockwise circle, back to the vine in the southwest corner, and climb back down to level six. From here, walk seven leaves

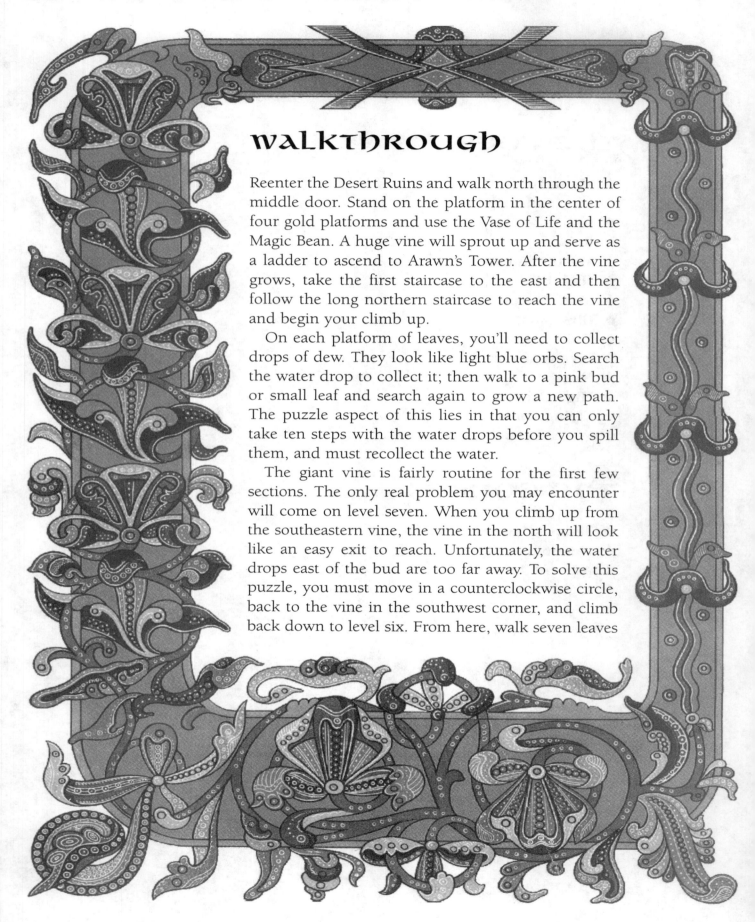

to the east and collect the water to use on the pink bud to the north. Climb up this vine to level seven and you'll be able to create a central walkway through the level, which will allow you to water the last pink bud. Climb this last vine to enter the Tower of Arawn.

In level one of the tower, walk through the northern doorway and then either east or west to reach the exit in the south.

On level two, you'll appear in the southern region of the map. Head in a clockwise circle to a room along the east wall to collect a Tempest Sword, and then wind back around in a counterclockwise quarter-circle to a doorway that leads to an exit in the center of the level.

On level three, the puzzle elements of the tower begin to kick in. Walk southwest over a sun symbol to the western wall and wind north along the path until you reach a door that leads outside. On the balcony, walk west until you reach the door with a moon symbol and enter. Now walk along the southwest path to the northernmost of two staircases.

On level four, walk north to the outer balcony. From here, travel east and collect the Hammer. Return to the moon door and walk along the southeast passage to the exit.

On level five, walk north and exit the moon door. On the balcony, travel west to the crack in the ground and use the Hammer. When the hole opens, drop down and walk east to the sun door. To return to level five, find the exit in the southeast corner. From here, walk a few steps northeast to reach level six.

On level six, walk out the south door to the balcony and head east to the moon door. Back inside, travel along the southwest edge of the level to reach the exit in the center of the room.

Upon reaching the final level, you'll find yourself in a small room with three gems on the wall. Touch the blue Gem of Elders to regain lost Magic Points. Touch the pink Gem of Vitality to regain lost Vitality Points. Then touch the green Gem of Life to resurrect any dead allies.

Arawn will appear, in the form of an old man, and tell you more about your mission. He will explain that the Underworld and the Common World must never meet, and that you must stop Bandore and the Vicious Ones from their evil intentions.

He'll give you an Ancient Tablet, which will guide you later in the journey, but you will be responsible for finding the other three tablets. He'll also provide each member with a Light Orb. When he's finished, he'll transport the team back to Simone.

SIMONE II

OBJECTIVES

You return to Simone to finally break the curse on Samson.

THE FOES

- ❖ **Ghost**
- ❖ **Roper**
- ❖ **Ork Lord**
- ❖ **Harpy**
- ❖ **Summoner**
- ❖ **Bandore Soldier**

THE GOODS

- ❖ **Wind Cloak**
- ❖ **Healing Herb**

WALKTHROUGH

You appear in the Mystic Shrine of Simone, courtesy of Arawn. At this point, Master Zeon will finally use his abilities to lift the curse on Samson. After a short ceremony, Samson will be as good as new and ready to prove himself in Zalagoon. From here, Zeon will leave to prepare the forces of Simone.

As you walk out of the shrine, search the treasure chest just southeast of the entrance, and you'll find a Wind Cloak for Edward. From here, you can proceed into town to replenish your supplies in the top floor of the inn. You'll probably want to purchase a few extra Mage's Potions for the battles ahead.

Though nothing really happens there, you can journey to the Mystic Tree. Inside, Zeon begins to rally his forces. When you're done, walk to the Mystic Shrine and take the northern path out of town. Slightly ahead and to the north, you'll find a cave opening that serves as a shortcut back to Zalagoon.

Enter the cave. The stairs to level two are in the northeast corner. Be sure to grab the Healing Herb in the treasure chest along the eastern wall. On the next level, travel to the northwest corner for the stairs up. On level three, continue to the northwestern corner of the area, and you'll run into a pair of Bandore

Soldiers who'll block the path. They'll give you the option to fight, so be prepared for a fairly tough battle if you accept. When the soldiers are defeated, exit the cave and head northeast to reach Zalagoon.

ZALAGOON II

OBJECTIVES

With Samson's curse finally broken, you return to Zalagoon to prove your identity to the royal family.

THE FOES

- ✣ **Illusionist**
- ✣ **Clay Golem**
- ✣ **Raise**
- ✣ **Imp**
- ✣ **Siren Harpy**
- ✣ **Dark Bishop**
- ✣ **Mystic Fungus**
- ✣ **Hell Hound**
- ✣ **Glade**

THE GOODS

- ❖ **Guiding Branch**
- ❖ **Iron Plate**
- ❖ **Cure Herb**
- ❖ **Music Box**
- ❖ **Ring of Power**

WALKTHROUGH

As you enter Zalagoon, you'll notice that there is a lack of activity. In fact, only the church and the inn are open for business. As you search the town, a young boy will inform you to meet Sir Bison at his quarters. At this point, Glade is close to convincing the king to surrender to Bandore.

To reach Bison, reenter the sewers and battle your way to the exit in the north. When you reach Bison, he'll instruct you to quickly head to the courtyard before Glade is successful. Be sure to take the stairs down from Bison's chamber to reach a treasure room with a Guiding Branch, Iron Plate, and Cure Herb.

In the courtyard, Samson will be given a second chance to prove his strength, and he'll succeed with flying colors. The king will finally accept the truth

and agree to send his forces to aid Marion. At this point, Glade will show his true colors, as a spy for the Bandore Army. He'll ingest a pill and transform into a monstrous creature who reveals that he has sold his soul to Lord Shutat. With Glade now a major Boss, this will not be an easy battle. Be sure to have some Mage's Potions in reserve, as you'll need to hit him with everything in your arsenal.

When Glade is defeated, the king will allow you to recuperate in the castle. When you awake in bed, search the western table before waking the others and you'll find the Music Box. From here, take the opportunity to search the castle. In the throne room, the king will ask for help in overthrowing the Bandore troops who guard the bridge to Marion. Take the stairs to the west of the king's throne and search the closet in the king's bedroom to find a Ring of Power.

Exit the castle and stop off in the city of Zalagoon. You'll be able to buy some advanced weapons and armor at the store to the west of the church. At this point, save your game and set off for Marion.

MARION KINGDOM II

OBJECTIVES

Clear the bridge and return to Marion to challenge the forces of Bandore and to rescue Prince Edward's father, the king.

THE FOES

- ✤ **Green Slime**
- ✤ **Flying Mouse**
- ✤ **Zombie**
- ✤ **Thief**
- ✤ **Giant Scorpion**
- ✤ **Bats**
- ✤ **Tumble Rabbit**
- ✤ **Killer Bee**
- ✤ **Dark Priest**
- ✤ **Ogre**
- ✤ **Evil Summoner**
- ✤ **Bandore Soldier**

the goods

- ❖ **Healing Herb**
- ❖ **Smoke Bomb**
- ❖ **Steel Key**
- ❖ **Tornado Card**
- ❖ **Thunder Card**
- ❖ **Mage's Potion**
- ❖ **Source of Defense**

walkthrough

With Glade defeated, you must now help the Zalagoon soldiers to return to Marion. Head southwest of Zalagoon to the bridge. It appears as if the Zalagoon forces are helpless to cross because of fortified Bandore troops on the western side. Because you won't be able to return via the bridge, head northwest of Zalagoon and enter Dragon Cave. The path through here is fairly straightforward, and the enemies are extremely weak. When you reach the small cavern opening, enter it and you'll find a house and a strange pair of tombstones bearing the names "Sir Norton" and "Lady Katherine." In the house, you will not be able to open the treasure chest yet, so

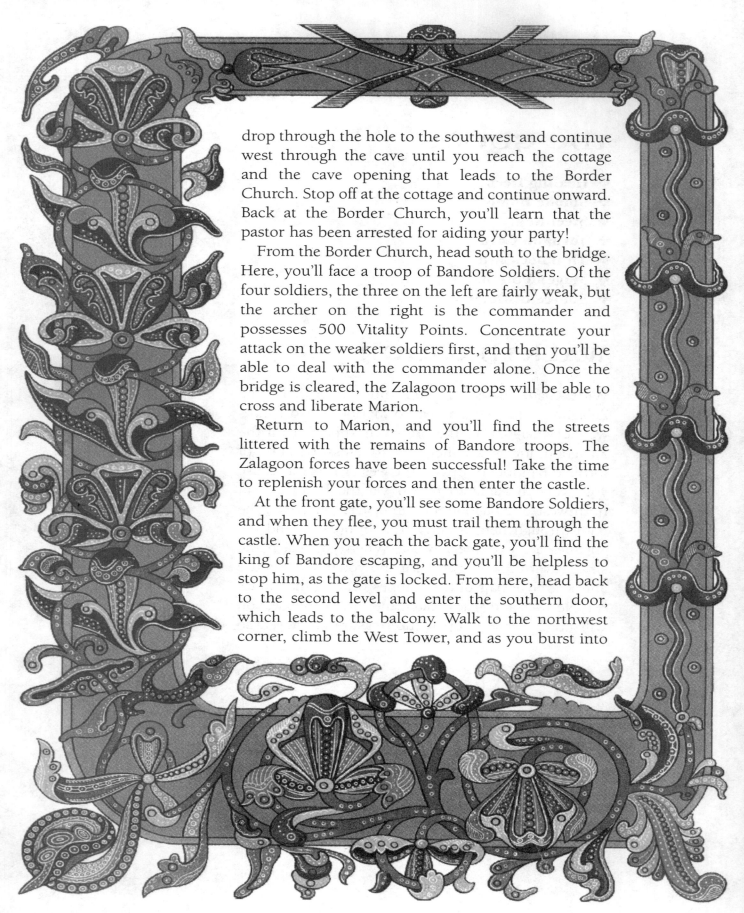

drop through the hole to the southwest and continue west through the cave until you reach the cottage and the cave opening that leads to the Border Church. Stop off at the cottage and continue onward. Back at the Border Church, you'll learn that the pastor has been arrested for aiding your party!

From the Border Church, head south to the bridge. Here, you'll face a troop of Bandore Soldiers. Of the four soldiers, the three on the left are fairly weak, but the archer on the right is the commander and possesses 500 Vitality Points. Concentrate your attack on the weaker soldiers first, and then you'll be able to deal with the commander alone. Once the bridge is cleared, the Zalagoon troops will be able to cross and liberate Marion.

Return to Marion, and you'll find the streets littered with the remains of Bandore troops. The Zalagoon forces have been successful! Take the time to replenish your forces and then enter the castle.

At the front gate, you'll see some Bandore Soldiers, and when they flee, you must trail them through the castle. When you reach the back gate, you'll find the king of Bandore escaping, and you'll be helpless to stop him, as the gate is locked. From here, head back to the second level and enter the southern door, which leads to the balcony. Walk to the northwest corner, climb the West Tower, and as you burst into

the room, you'll find that Ramue is placing a cursed mask on a man. She'll send some goons after you, and disappear. Defeat these enemies, and you'll collect the Steel Key. Walk to the eastern edge of the balcony and use the Steel Key to open the East Tower. You'll find Edward's father, the king, and his advisor safely imprisoned. Now travel back to the back gate and use the Steel Key to open it. The key hole is on the left side.

At this point, you'll enter a forced event mode of the Bandore king escaping without Shutat or Ramue, who appear too late. They figure they may as well deal with your party now, but as they turn to destroy you, the combined forces of Marion and Zalagoon appear to save the day and drive off the enemies.

Return to the king's throne room. As a reward for saving the kingdom, the king will allow you to raid the treasury. When you're done here, search the treasure chests throughout the castle to find a Tornado Card, Thunder Card, Mage's Potion, and Source of Defense.

Unfortunately, you'll also learn that Sir Kevins has been kidnapped by the Bandore Army. Edward wants to invade Bandore, but the king says the time is not right and orders Edward and Samson to remain in Marion. With your forces depleted, you now must head west on the road to Bandore to rescue Sir Kevins.

BANDORE

OBJECTIVES

Now that Marion has been liberated of Bandore's forces, it's time to take the battle to them. In Bandore, you'll have to find a piece of the Ancient Tablet, as well as save Sir Kevins.

THE FOES

- **Hell Hound**
- **Ogre**
- **Clay Golem**
- **Dark Bishop**
- **Fire Giant**
- **Bandore Soldier**
- **Evil Summoner**
- **Razor Demon**
- **Phantom Armor**
- **Wyvern**
- **Stone Golem**
- **Pyro-Hydra**

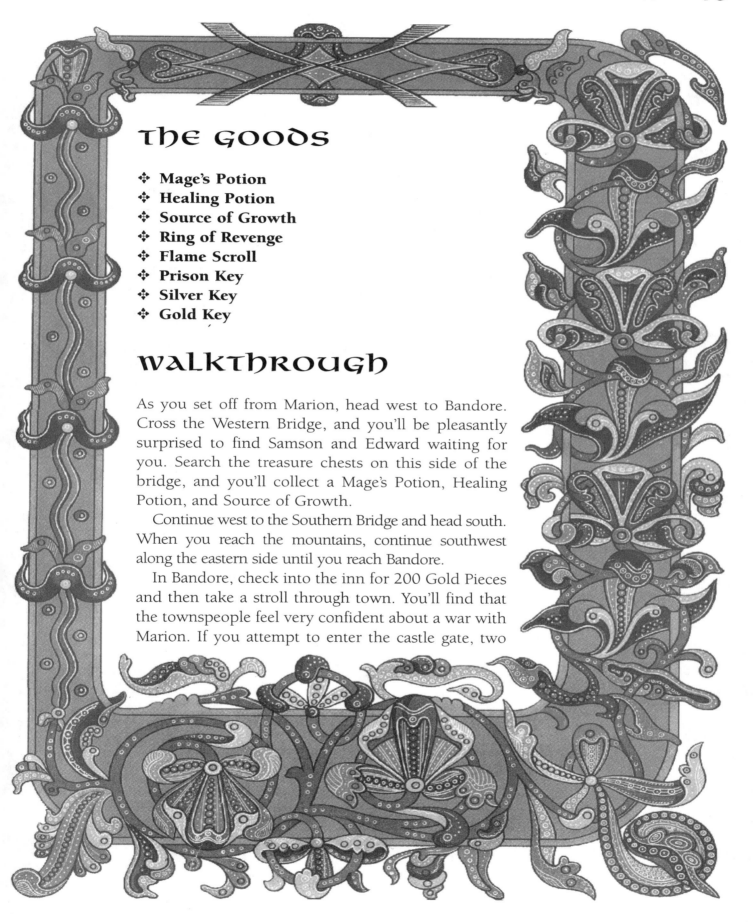

THE GOODS

- ❖ **Mage's Potion**
- ❖ **Healing Potion**
- ❖ **Source of Growth**
- ❖ **Ring of Revenge**
- ❖ **Flame Scroll**
- ❖ **Prison Key**
- ❖ **Silver Key**
- ❖ **Gold Key**

WALKTHROUGH

As you set off from Marion, head west to Bandore. Cross the Western Bridge, and you'll be pleasantly surprised to find Samson and Edward waiting for you. Search the treasure chests on this side of the bridge, and you'll collect a Mage's Potion, Healing Potion, and Source of Growth.

Continue west to the Southern Bridge and head south. When you reach the mountains, continue southwest along the eastern side until you reach Bandore.

In Bandore, check into the inn for 200 Gold Pieces and then take a stroll through town. You'll find that the townspeople feel very confident about a war with Marion. If you attempt to enter the castle gate, two

troops will deny you entrance. Talk to everyone you can, and you'll hear rumors of a secret entrance into the castle. If you approach the house in the northwest corner of town, you'll view a forced event mode of a worried mother instructing her son to sneak some food into the castle through the secret entrance. He'll take the food, via a hole in the western wall of the city. If you enter the house and search the vase in the southeast corner, you'll find the Ring of Revenge.

Now that you have a means to enter the castle, make sure you are absolutely prepared before setting off into the next part of the adventure. Once you take the secret entrance, you'll face a number of tough enemies and will have to travel a long way before reaching another save or rest point, so stock up and be sure to use your supplies wisely.

When you're ready, enter the hole in the western wall and travel south to find a secret cave opening outside the city limits. In the cave, take a few steps west and then head due north. A few screen-lengths ahead, you'll come to a fork in the road. If you head northwest, you'll find a treasure chest with a Flame Scroll. From here, head back to the fork and go northeast to the cave exit.

This exit will allow you into the castle basement. Although it appears that you are boxed in by vases, you can actually walk along the southern wall to explore the room. The door in the northwest corner

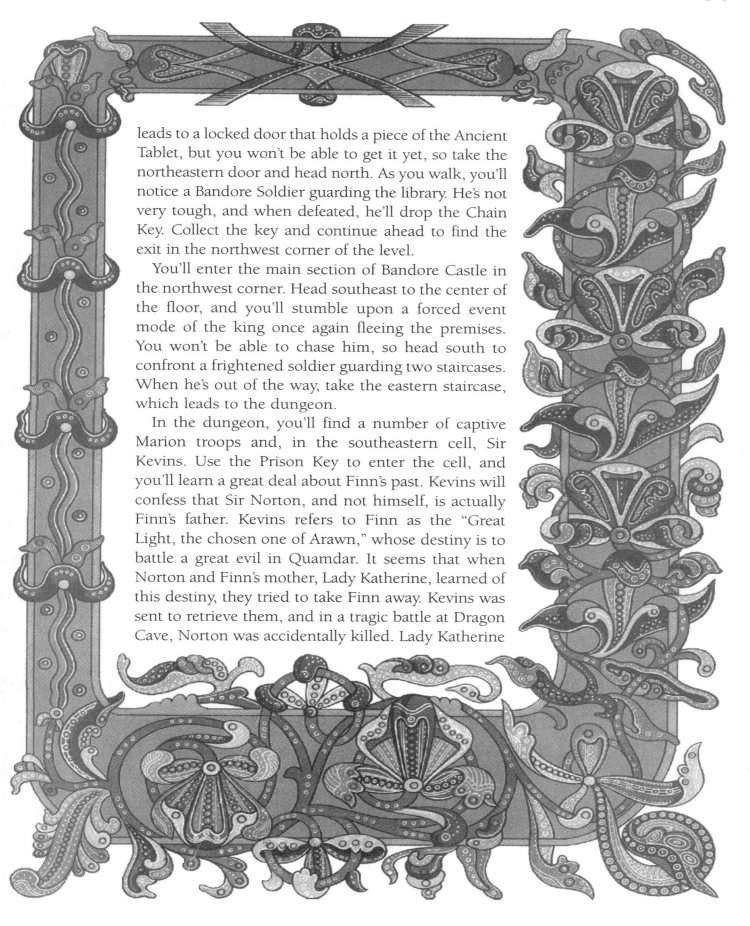

leads to a locked door that holds a piece of the Ancient Tablet, but you won't be able to get it yet, so take the northeastern door and head north. As you walk, you'll notice a Bandore Soldier guarding the library. He's not very tough, and when defeated, he'll drop the Chain Key. Collect the key and continue ahead to find the exit in the northwest corner of the level.

You'll enter the main section of Bandore Castle in the northwest corner. Head southeast to the center of the floor, and you'll stumble upon a forced event mode of the king once again fleeing the premises. You won't be able to chase him, so head south to confront a frightened soldier guarding two staircases. When he's out of the way, take the eastern staircase, which leads to the dungeon.

In the dungeon, you'll find a number of captive Marion troops and, in the southeastern cell, Sir Kevins. Use the Prison Key to enter the cell, and you'll learn a great deal about Finn's past. Kevins will confess that Sir Norton, and not himself, is actually Finn's father. Kevins refers to Finn as the "Great Light, the chosen one of Arawn," whose destiny is to battle a great evil in Quamdar. It seems that when Norton and Finn's mother, Lady Katherine, learned of this destiny, they tried to take Finn away. Kevins was sent to retrieve them, and in a tragic battle at Dragon Cave, Norton was accidentally killed. Lady Katherine

became comatose, and soon died as well. To honor Finn's parents, Kevins buried them in the cave and raised the child as his own. These are the tombstones you saw in Dragon Cave. Kevins will implore you to go, and as you leave, Bandore troops will appear to drag Kevins off to his execution at the Volcano.

To save him, take the stairs up, and on the main floor of the castle, climb the western staircase. You'll wind up in the king's chamber, but for now there's no time to explore. Head south to the balcony, and then east to the Volcano Cliffs. Continue along the path until you reach a section where Ramue and Shutat will trap you and force you to battle their pets. When the enemies are defeated, you'll still be trapped, until a mysterious masked figure tosses a Silver Key in your direction. Collect it, and use it to open the southeast door. From here, continue on the path northeast until you find a staircase and an opening to the Volcano Caves.

In the caves, the levels are not long, but they are filled with dangerous enemies and patches of lava that can drain your health if you step on them. On level one, you'll start in the southwest corner. Walk north and then east to reach the stairs in the northeast corner. On level two, you'll begin in the direct center of the cave. From here, walk to the northeast corner and then due south to find the exit along the border of the level. On level three, walk along the southern

wall and take the second northern passage. Unfortunately, you'll be forced to take some damage by crossing the lava here, but if you're quick, it should be minimal. The exit can be found in the northeast corner. The fourth and last level starts you in the southern region of the map. Travel west and continue along the path as it loops to the northeastern section of the cave. This will take you back outside the caves.

Fresh air never looked so good, but don't relax just yet! Continue to journey northeast until you reach the first staircase, then to the west and the second staircase, and finally back east again to the third set of stairs. As you descend each group of stairs, you'll hear the wail of a tortured Kevins. When you reach him, he'll hang perilously over the lava and beg for your help. As you move to untie the rope and help him, you'll discover that it was an elaborate ruse by the evil magician Yeon. He'll turn the tables on you, and you'll be the one hanging for dear life. Out of nowhere, Kevins will appear to save you. Unfortunately, it will cost him his life. Though you feel down, Arawn will appear and remind you that you must continue on.

Enter the cave just east of the pulley, cross the lava, and collect the Gold Key. Now you must journey all the way back through the Volcano Caves. Once through the caves, pass the staircase that led to the opening and continue on the western path until you reach a locked door. Use the Gold Key to open the door, enter the cave, and head to the northwest section until you reach the dock.

On the dock, the king of Bandore will find himself betrayed by Ramue and Shutat. They've left him high and dry, and to add injury to insult, they attack him with their ship's cannons. When he is dead, they plan to add you to their hit list, but a mysterious dragon prevents them from carrying out their objective. They quickly head off for Barbaros, and as you leave the dock, Domino reappears. He'll join the team and later allow you to use his ship to follow the others. Walk south and back into the castle. Don't forget to return to the locked door in the basement to collect the Ancient Tablet. The Gold Key will unlock the door. Now head back to town and save your game!

Leave

OBJECTIVES

Set sail with Domino to track Ramue and Shutat. On your voyage, stop off in Leave to replenish your supplies and to gain information about Barbaros.

THE FOES

- **Minotaur**
- **Vampire Worm**
- **Vampire Bat**
- **Evil Summoner**
- **Mirage Dragon**
- **Razor Demons**
- **Venom Giant**
- **Dark Bishop**

THE GOODS

- **World Map**

WALKTHROUGH

Rest up, then return to Domino's ship at the dock. Before talking to Domino, search the ship, specifically the table in Domino's quarters. You'll collect a World Map. If you take the time to read some books in his library, you'll learn that he is seeking to avenge his family. With the map in hand, talk to Domino. He'll insist that you drop one member of the party so that

he may join. The decision is up to you, so once you make it, you'll be on your way.

In the ship, travel northwest along the edge of the volcano and then south along the eastern coastline. When you reach the green, grassy area, dock the ship and walk south to Leave.

In Leave, it will cost 200 Gold Pieces to rest at the inn. If you talk to the townspeople, you'll hear about a castle in the Northwest called Barbaros. With this information, load up on supplies and prepare to set sail.

On Domino's ship, head west along the cape and then continue up the coast. Pass the first waterway inland and continue up until you reach the second one. Follow this waterway to the east, through the upper fork until you reach the forest. Dock the ship and walk north and then southeast until you reach Barbaros.

BARBAROS CASTLE

OBJECTIVES

You enter Barbaros in hopes of finding Ramue and Shutat, but instead discover a true warrior princess, as well as a section of the Ancient Tablet.

THE FOES

None.

THE GOODS

None.

WALKTHROUGH

Your first trip to Barbaros will not be very eventful, but there are a few things you'll discover.

First off, the general atmosphere is that of a very rough place. This is definitely a warrior's town. In the courtyard, you'll get your first look at Lorele in action. She is the king's daughter and a definite warrior in her own right. You won't be able to add her to your party until your return trip later, so don't bother looking for her now.

When you meet the king, he'll refuse to hear you out unless you can prove yourselves capable heroes on Discipline Island. If you're observant, you'll probably notice the Ancient Tablet section that adorns the wall behind his throne.

When you've restocked your equipment and saved your game, press on to Discipline Island. It can be found offshore, east of Leave.

DISCIPLINE ISLAND

OBJECTIVES

Enter the Shrine of Discipline to face a challenge of your heroic abilities.

THE FOES

- ❖ **Evil Summoner**
- ❖ **Huge Gel**
- ❖ **Venom Giant**
- ❖ **Succubus**

THE GOODS

- ❖ **Source of Courage**
- ❖ **Source of Power**

- ❖ **Blizzard Scroll**
- ❖ **Mystic Blade**

WALKTHROUGH

On the island, stop off to rest at the inn before facing the trials ahead. The cost will be 250 Gold Pieces, but it will be well worth it to be completely refreshed before your trial. In the southwest house, search the vase for a Healing Potion. In the northwest house, you'll meet a friendly girl who will offer an invitation to return after you complete the test. If you search her house, you'll find a Source of Courage.

When you're ready, walk along the northern path to the Shrine of Discipline. In the shrine, search the vase in the room in the southeast corner to find a Blizzard Scroll.

At the northern end of the shrine, a man in a purple robe will ask if you are ready to test yourself. If you've loaded Finn up with supplies, and feel your ready, accept the challenge. You'll find yourself in a room with various shapes made up of colored tiles. The key here is to memorize the patterns and then climb the staircase to the second floor. Here, the floor is transparent, except for a few symbol tiles. Now, when you step on a colored-symbol tile, the corresponding shape will briefly flash in a quick outline of safe steps. Walk along these safe steps to collect the different items. On a ledge along the northwestern wall, you'll find a Source of Power.

The following are the necessary path steps to reach the Mystic Blade. Stand on the first orange tile. Take five steps north and one step west to the green tile. Next, take one step north and five steps east to the purple tile. Now go one step north, one step west, one step north, one step west, three steps north, and one step west to the green tile. Next, go one step north, four steps east, one step north, two steps east, and two steps south. This should leave you just west of the treasure chest with no ledge. Search the chest to collect the Mystic Blade.

With the blade in hand, you'll be transported back to the shrine and will be promoted to Hero. In addition, all party members who have reached level twenty or higher will also be eligible for promotion. If your party members have not reached level twenty yet, you can always return later in the game to promote them, when they are ready.

Return to the town and visit with your fan in the northwest house. She'll get you drunk and ask you to consider settling on the island. As you leave the town, you'll be surprised to see that Steiner has been promoted, as well, and can now transport the party through the air. Climb aboard, by standing next to him and pressing the $\boxed{\text{X}}$, and head back to Barbaros.

BARBAROS CASTLE II

OBJECTIVES

Return to Barbaros to prove your worth to the king. You'll find a city in ruins, and you'll be able to collect the third Ancient Tablet section and perhaps a new member.

THE FOES

None.

THE GOODS

- ✣ **Thunder Scroll**
- ✣ **Bronze Key**
- ✣ **War Rod**
- ✣ **Wind Bandanna**
- ✣ **Healing Jewel**

WALKTHROUGH

When you return to Barbaros, you'll find the city in ruins. Apparently, Ramue and Shutat unleashed the fury of their ship's cannons, and as a result many of the townspeople and soldiers lie dead.

In the throne room, you'll witness the last moments of the king's life. He'll ramble a few words about Ramue, Spirit Water, and Lorele, and then kick the bucket. At this point, collect the Ancient Tablet on the wall behind the throne. In the eastern hall, walk to the dark room, northeast of the priest's room. Upon entry, the room will light up, and a frightened soldier will hand you a Bronze Key. Walk down the northern stairs and unlock the door to release Lorele. She'll dash off, but don't be in a hurry to pursue her. Instead, open the three treasure chests to find a War Rod, a Wind Bandanna, and a Healing Jewel. Now return to the throne room, and after Lorele pays her last respects to her father, she'll join the team for revenge. She'll instruct you to meet her outside, and when you do, you'll have to drop a party member.

As you continue to search the castle, you'll discover a few more things. On the second floor, search a vase in the northwest corner of the balcony to find a Thunder Scroll. From there, walk straight south down the western wall, and then east to the far tower in the southeast corner. Stand under the tower and talk to find a hidden merchant with some great exclusive items, such as the Unicorn Horn, Angel's Ocarina, Reviving Herb, and Slow Card.

When your team is set, take Steiner in search of the last missing piece of the Ancient Tablet.

PITY ISLAND

OBJECTIVES

Venture through the mazes of Pity Island to collect the fourth and final section of the Ancient Tablet.

THE FOES

- ❖ **Basilik**
- ❖ **Griffin**
- ❖ **Black Aerial**
- ❖ **Dark Elf**
- ❖ **Evil Shaman**

- ❖ Burial
- ❖ Poltergeist
- ❖ Wight
- ❖ Fenril
- ❖ Hippogriff
- ❖ Manticore

THE GOODS

- ❖ Mage's Jewel
- ❖ Power Knuckles
- ❖ Throwing Knife
- ❖ Ancient Tablet

WALKTHROUGH

Your next destination is Pity Island. You'll find it in the waters off the continent's shores, south of Isla.

On land, enter the temple. You'll notice that each cave is filled with red and green mushrooms. Touch the green mushrooms to shrink and the red mushrooms to restore your size to normal. In many sections, you'll be forced to temporarily shrink to slip through cracks, ride leaves, etc.

Inside the first section of caves, walk north and then east. In the first southern passage, you'll find a treasure chest with a Mage's Jewel. From here, head north to return to the eastern tunnel and continue to the exit in the southeast corner.

On level two, walk north, touch the green mushroom to shrink, and pass through the crack in the western chamber. You'll find the exit ladder to the north.

On the third level, look for the green mushroom against the western wall and carefully walk in a counterclockwise circle along the outer wall to reach the crack in the northeastern wall. If you slip and touch a red mushroom, you'll have to start the puzzle over.

On the fourth level, touch a green mushroom and drop through the hole in the northwest corner to collect the Power Knuckles from the treasure chest on level three. Ride the leaf back across the water and return to level four. The exit can be found in the southwest corner.

On level five, you have the option to take the northern ladder out or shrink and head to the southeast corner to collect the Throwing Knife. If you choose the latter, head north to the exit ladder.

On the sixth level, things begin to get tricky. Shrink down, ride the leaf east, drop down the

southeastern hole, and head to the northern ladder. From here, touch the green mushroom to the east and walk through the opening in the north wall. Ride the southwest leaf to the west and then take the next leaf you pass to the far eastern side of the room. Walk north to the ladder to level eight.

On level eight, touch a green mushroom and ride the next two leaves north to the Ancient Tablet. Collect the tablet from the wall and use the Guiding Branch to exit back outside.

Outside the caves, you'll now have all four pieces of the Ancient Tablet and will soon be able to raise the Ocean Pyramid.

OCEAN PYRAMID

OBJECTIVES

Use the four sections of the Ancient Tablet to restore the Ocean Pyramid.

THE FOES

- ✤ **Ekidona**
- ✤ **Hippogriff**
- ✤ **Burial**
- ✤ **Manticore**
- ✤ **Fenril**
- ✤ **Minotaur Lord**
- ✤ **Green Dragon**
- ✤ **Evil Shaman**
- ✤ **Stone Golem**

THE GOODS

- ✤ **Devil's Ribbon**
- ✤ **Battle Shield**
- ✤ **Torch**
- ✤ **Silk Scarf**

WALKTHROUGH

From Pity Island, fly with Steiner to the four small islands north of Discipline Island. You'll find a small temple and a guardian on each island. Talk to each

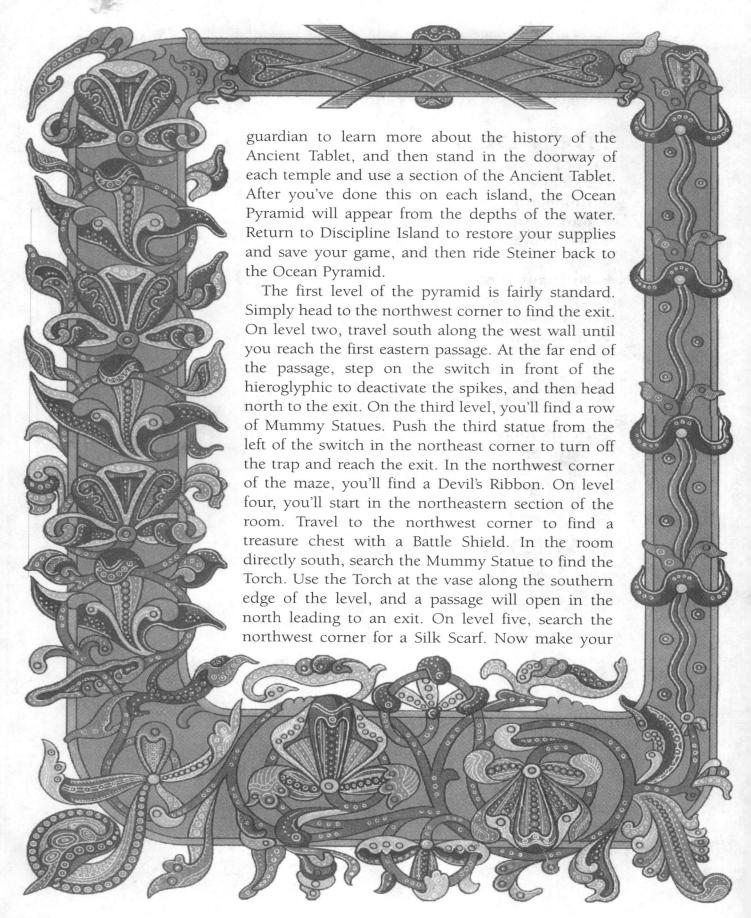

guardian to learn more about the history of the Ancient Tablet, and then stand in the doorway of each temple and use a section of the Ancient Tablet. After you've done this on each island, the Ocean Pyramid will appear from the depths of the water. Return to Discipline Island to restore your supplies and save your game, and then ride Steiner back to the Ocean Pyramid.

The first level of the pyramid is fairly standard. Simply head to the northwest corner to find the exit. On level two, travel south along the west wall until you reach the first eastern passage. At the far end of the passage, step on the switch in front of the hieroglyphic to deactivate the spikes, and then head north to the exit. On the third level, you'll find a row of Mummy Statues. Push the third statue from the left of the switch in the northeast corner to turn off the trap and reach the exit. In the northwest corner of the maze, you'll find a Devil's Ribbon. On level four, you'll start in the northeastern section of the room. Travel to the northwest corner to find a treasure chest with a Battle Shield. In the room directly south, search the Mummy Statue to find the Torch. Use the Torch at the vase along the southern edge of the level, and a passage will open in the north leading to an exit. On level five, search the northwest corner for a Silk Scarf. Now make your way around the numerous spike traps and exit in the southeast corner. On the sixth level, walk to the northeast corner and move the statue onto the switch to the immediate left. In the next passage, push the second statue north to block the Lion Statue's fire-breath. To the east of this room, you'll find an exit. The seventh and final level is fairly easy. Simply push the three statues onto their respective switches, and the center chamber will open.

As you enter the chamber, a forced event mode will begin showing a warship harpooning the Ocean Pyramid to anchor it down. Steiner will battle the ship of the Vicious Ones and its leader Dagoot, but he'll be shot by a magic arrow. In one last heroic act, he'll defeat Dagoot and release the Ocean Pyramid from its anchor. Unable to stay aloft, he'll plunge to the ocean depths to his apparent death. Although sad, the party realizes it must go on.

To that end, you can now use the Ocean Pyramid to travel throughout the land. If you take some time to survey the lands, you'll find a valley in the mountains between Zalagoon and Marion which was previously inaccessible. Land the ship and enter the temple.

Within the Dragon Shrine, you'll learn of your need to find the fifth section of the Ancient Tablet to open the path to the Abyss. To your surprise, you'll also find Steiner safely being tended to. He'll be

waiting for you in Isla, should you have further need of him. Now it's off to find the missing piece of the puzzle.

MISTRAL/THE FIFTH TEMPLE

OBJECTIVES

As you search for the fifth temple, stop off in Mistral to prepare yourself for the battle for the final section of the Ancient Tablet. The final piece to the puzzle will soon be yours.

THE FOES

- ✜ **Necromancer**
- ✜ **Lich**
- ✜ **Dagoot**

THE GOODS

+ **Mystic Staff**
+ **Final Tablet**
+ **Seraphic Ring**

WALKTHROUGH

As you go exploring with the Ocean Pyramid, head to the northwest corner of the land. Along the northern coast you'll find the city of Mistral.

In the city, you'll find an industrious race of dwarves. The blacksmith will offer to forge some weapons for you if you will venture to the eastern mountains and enter the ice caves to retrieve some Mithril. This mission is entirely optional, and has no bearing on the main adventure of the game.

Take the opportunity to prepare your team, and when you're ready, head northwest in the pyramid. You'll find the fifth temple on this small island. Set the pyramid down and enter the temple.

Walk north to the row of torches and search the first torch west, of the red carpet, to collect the Magic Staff. In the northeast corner, a torch blocks the entrance to a door. Stand to the left of the torch and perform a search to push it out of the way. Descend

down each flight of stairs until you reach the bottom of the temple.

At the lowest level, you'll find Dagoot and his goons waiting for you. Take the fight to them, and the path to the Final Tablet will be cleared. Although Dagoot possesses some fearsome magic, he and his forces should be no match for your troops. Once he is defeated, climb the platform and collect the Final Tablet.

Do you see the room to the east of the platform with a treasure chest, but no door? To enter, search the wall in the northwest corner of the room, and you'll discover a secret pathway that winds behind the main room and leads to a Seraphic Ring.

With the tablet in hand, exit the temple and take to the skies once again.

ZEAL

OBJECTIVES

The road to Quamdar begins in Zeal. Journey through the Sand Caves to reach the hometown of Shutat.

the foes

- ❖ **Lich**
- ❖ **Young Dragon**
- ❖ **Necromancer**
- ❖ **Demon**
- ❖ **Demon's Pet**
- ❖ **Dead Armor**
- ❖ **Undead Knight**
- ❖ **Bat**
- ❖ **Black Knight**

the goods

- ❖ **Evil Armor**
- ❖ **Source of Magic**
- ❖ **Drain Rod**
- ❖ **Mystic Dagger**
- ❖ **Healing Jewel**
- ❖ **Source of Vitality**
- ❖ **Shadow Gi**
- ❖ **Thunder Vase**

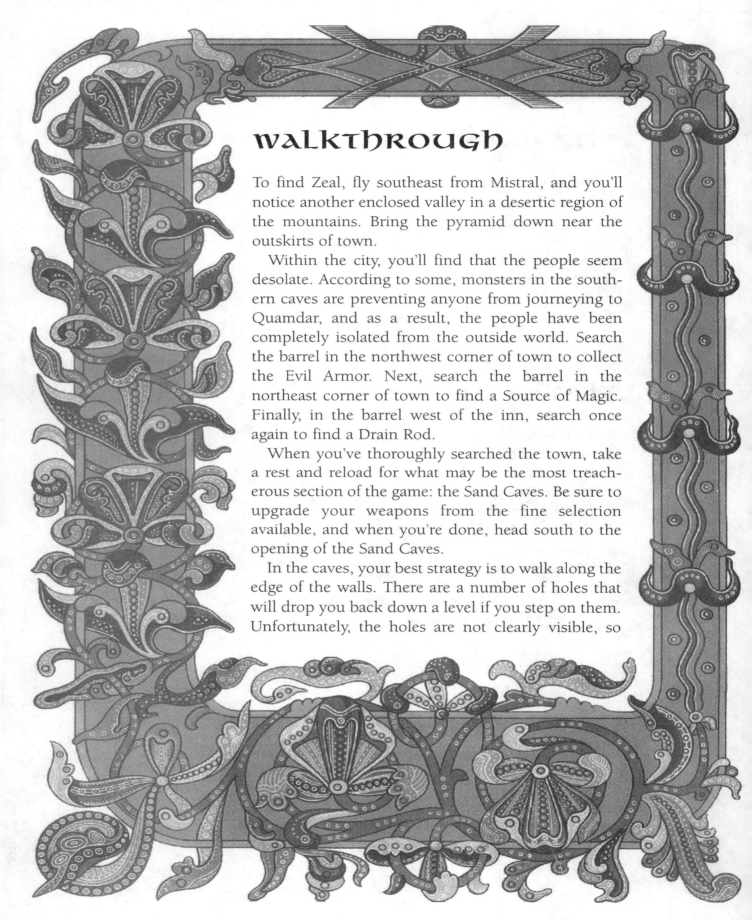

WALKTHROUGH

To find Zeal, fly southeast from Mistral, and you'll notice another enclosed valley in a desertic region of the mountains. Bring the pyramid down near the outskirts of town.

Within the city, you'll find that the people seem desolate. According to some, monsters in the southern caves are preventing anyone from journeying to Quamdar, and as a result, the people have been completely isolated from the outside world. Search the barrel in the northwest corner of town to collect the Evil Armor. Next, search the barrel in the northeast corner of town to find a Source of Magic. Finally, in the barrel west of the inn, search once again to find a Drain Rod.

When you've thoroughly searched the town, take a rest and reload for what may be the most treacherous section of the game: the Sand Caves. Be sure to upgrade your weapons from the fine selection available, and when you're done, head south to the opening of the Sand Caves.

In the caves, your best strategy is to walk along the edge of the walls. There are a number of holes that will drop you back down a level if you step on them. Unfortunately, the holes are not clearly visible, so

you'll have to rely on your memorization skills to progress. Another common obstacle will be the Sand Monsters who will spring up from the ground to block your path. They won't attack, but they will make it more difficult to get around.

In level one, you'll begin in the southeast corner and must simply travel to the southwest corner of the map to exit.

On the next level, walk to the southern edge of the cave to find stairs to a cavern that holds a Mystic Dagger. Return to the main cave and walk along the eastern wall to the northeast corner and, finally, the exit in the northwest corner. The treasure chest south of the exit holds a Healing Jewel.

On level three, walk south through the thin southern passage, then northeast, and then south along the eastern wall. The exit lies in the southeast corner. In the center of the cave, look for a treasure chest with a Source of Vitality.

In the fourth cave, head due south to the edge of the level. From here, walk east along the wall and continue north until you reach a fork in the road. Choose the northwest path to find the exit.

On the fifth level, walk east along the northern wall, slowly bearing south. At the first lake, walk through the center and head for the far eastern wall.

Walk north along the wall and continue until you reach the exit in the northwest cavern. In a passage to the far west, you'll find a Shadow Gi, if you choose to look.

On level six, look for a treasure chest in the mid-southern region with a Thunder Vase. The exit to this level can be found in the southwest corner, so simply travel southeast to the southern edge and walk west along the wall to reach it.

Before you reach the exit, you'll have to face the Black Knight. As far as Bosses go, he's fairly easy to defeat, but this is an intriguing situation. It seems that the Black Knight is actually a brainwashed Percy, and the mysterious figure who's helped you on more than one occasion. You can either choose to battle him—in which case, he will die at the conclusion of the battle, despite his sister Annie's best efforts—or you can refuse to fight, and run each time he attacks you until he eventually breaks the hold the curse has on him. When the curse is broken, Percy will be eligible to rejoin the team.

After this battle, exit the caves and head for Quamdar.

QUAMDAR

OBJECTIVES

The end is close, and Quamdar will be your last chance to prepare for the final challenges ahead.

THE FOES

None

THE GOODS

- ✤ **Gundalf Hood**
- ✤ **Skeleton Key**
- ✤ **Dragon Blade**
- ✤ **Reviving Herb**
- ✤ **Tornado Vase**

WALKTHROUGH

To reach Quamdar, travel southeast between the waterways.

In town, enjoy a hard-earned rest at the inn for 500 Gold Pieces, and then search the town. The weapon selection here is top-notch so buy the best for the final showdown, which you will soon encounter.

Talking with the townspeople, you may be surprised to learn that Shutat was not always so evil. In fact, he seems to enjoy quite a following around the city. You'll learn how he ended up as an evil tool of the Vicious Ones. If you search the barrel in the house in the northwestern corner, you'll find a Gundalf Hood.

When you're finished in Quamdar, step outside the city limits and use the Light Orb. You'll be allowed to transport to any town in which a previously deployed member of the team resides. This will allow you restock on any items you may be missing or to realign your forces for the journey to the Abyss. With Steiner, the pyramid, and the boat at your disposal, there is one last critical journey you must take. Return to Dragon Cave and venture to the area where you first saw the sleeping dragon. The lights will dim, and after a brief coming-of-age ceremony for Finn, you'll be able to collect the Skeleton Key. Travel to the secret cavern with the tombstones and unlock the treasure chest in the house. You'll gain the Dragon Blade. The Skeleton Key may be used to open any previously locked door you may have encountered along the way. Return to the Bandore dungeon to collect a Reviving Herb, and then go back to the Mystic Tree to collect the Tornado Vase from the locked rooms.

When you're finally prepared, return to Quamdar to face the ultimate evil!

The Abyss

Objectives

The time has come for a final confrontation with the Lord of Evil. There are four Boss characters in the Abyss, so keep a Guiding Branch handy. You should also stock up on Mage's Potions and Healing Potions. Remember that Healing Potions work much better than Healing Herbs.

THE FOES

- Necromancer
- Red Dragon
- Shadow Dragon
- Nightmare Queen
- Barog
- Demon
- Greater Demon
- Undead Lector
- Royal Guard
- Hydra Warrior
- Royal Guard
- Yeon
- Ramue
- Shutat
- Akkadias

THE GOODS

- Hero Scale

WALKTHROUGH

When you first enter the Abyss, you will walk past two priests. Yeon awaits at the northern part of the room.

Yeon has 1,150 Vitality Points and two cronies with him: a Hydra Warrior and a Royal Guard. Start by casting powerful spells that affect all three characters. You'll want to defeat his cronies in the first round, if possible. Once fat boy is all by himself, go to work. Use the Attack Spell on Finn and Samson, and bombard Yeon with your toughest spells. He isn't too tough, so you should have no problem. If you barely win this battle, you may want to boost your characters' levels. Now you can use the Last Tablet on the indentation in the floor at the northern end of the room. After you defeat Peon, or was it Yeon, you should return to town and restock your items. Was it that obvious that Yeon has never had a date in his life?

In this maze, your goal is to take two orbs from two statues and deliver them to their "sister" statues deeper in the maze. There are Light Statues–Angels, and Dark Statues–Skeletons. There are also two orbs–the Light Orb and the Dark Orb. All you have to do is deliver the orbs. Sounds simple, doesn't it? Here's the catch: You can only carry one of the orbs

at a time. When you have the Light Orb, all of the Dark Statues will emit a force field. Many of these fields block doorways and stairwells. The opposite is true with the Dark Orb. So, let's get started.

Once you have used the Last Tablet, you may exit this room through the northern doorway. You will now be in a room with four statues: two Light, on the left; two Dark, on the right. Enter the stairwell to the north, and you will be in a room shaped like a backwards "C." Go east to the hallway. Once you reach the hallway, go north. Enter the portal at the northern end of the room. Travel through the round room until you reach the doorway on the opposite side and go through.

You are now in the orb room. Examine the Angel to take the Light Orb. Notice how the Dark Statues glow. Spooky, huh? Exit this room the way you came in, and travel back through the round room. You'll find yourself back in the backwards "C" room. Go east to the hallway, then south. Go west and take the stairwell on the left. Notice that the steps are going down. Remember that you are in the Underworld, so down is good!

Now you are in a room shaped like a backwards "E." You will start in the middle. There are eight statues in the room: four Light and four Dark, in a zigzag pattern. Travel to the southern stairwell. Go east to the hallway, south past four statues, and then west to the stairwell. Notice these steps are going down!

You are now in the southern end of a square-shaped room. You'll want to take the portal to the north. To get there, go west until you see a hallway with two Light statues. Travel north to a larger room and enter the portal. You will pass through another round room.

When you exit the round room, you will be at the southern end of a room with many pillars. Go north through any hallway to a room full of statues. Take the stairwell to the northeast. You will have to walk past the Dark Statues. Notice that the stairwell is going down!

Now you will be in the northeast corner of a room with many pillars. Head south through the hallway and take the stairwell (going down) in the center of the room.

You will now be in the center of a large room with six Light Statues to the south. Walk past the Light Statues and enter the portal at the southern end of the room. Go through the round room.

You should be at the northern end of a large room. Make your way to the stairwell (going down) in the center of the room. It is the only stairwell in the room!

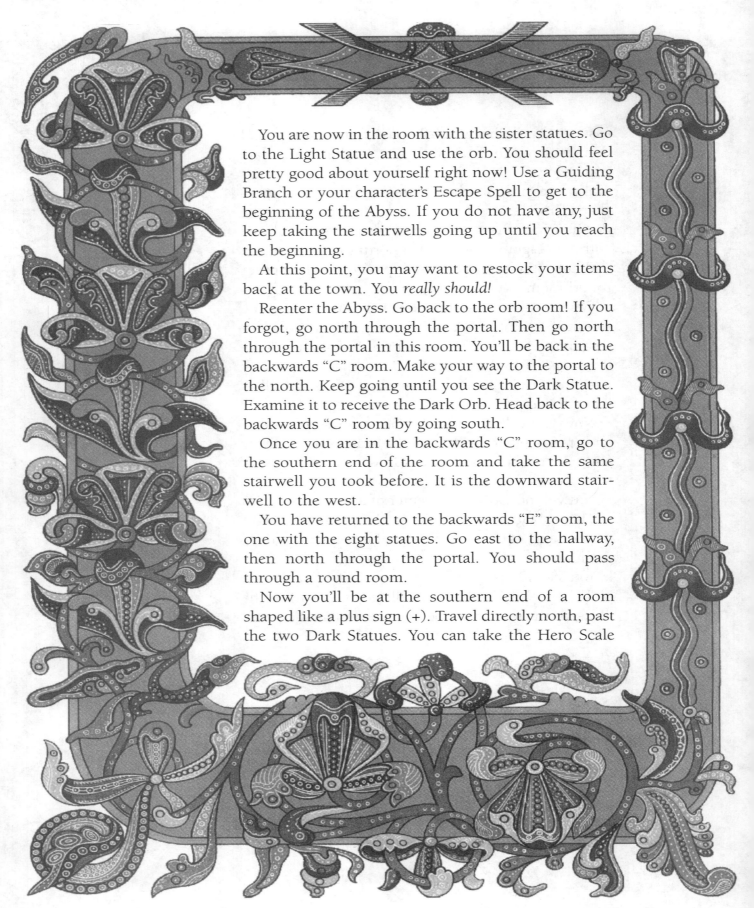

You are now in the room with the sister statues. Go to the Light Statue and use the orb. You should feel pretty good about yourself right now! Use a Guiding Branch or your character's Escape Spell to get to the beginning of the Abyss. If you do not have any, just keep taking the stairwells going up until you reach the beginning.

At this point, you may want to restock your items back at the town. You *really should!*

Reenter the Abyss. Go back to the orb room! If you forgot, go north through the portal. Then go north through the portal in this room. You'll be back in the backwards "C" room. Make your way to the portal to the north. Keep going until you see the Dark Statue. Examine it to receive the Dark Orb. Head back to the backwards "C" room by going south.

Once you are in the backwards "C" room, go to the southern end of the room and take the same stairwell you took before. It is the downward stairwell to the west.

You have returned to the backwards "E" room, the one with the eight statues. Go east to the hallway, then north through the portal. You should pass through a round room.

Now you'll be at the southern end of a room shaped like a plus sign (+). Travel directly north, past the two Dark Statues. You can take the Hero Scale

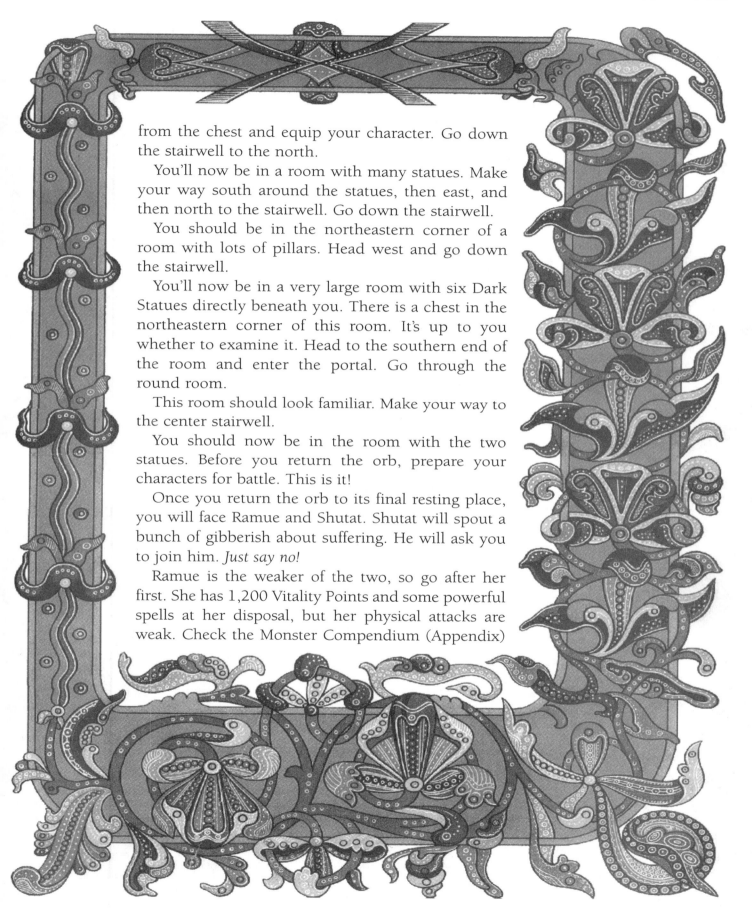

from the chest and equip your character. Go down the stairwell to the north.

You'll now be in a room with many statues. Make your way south around the statues, then east, and then north to the stairwell. Go down the stairwell.

You should be in the northeastern corner of a room with lots of pillars. Head west and go down the stairwell.

You'll now be in a very large room with six Dark Statues directly beneath you. There is a chest in the northeastern corner of this room. It's up to you whether to examine it. Head to the southern end of the room and enter the portal. Go through the round room.

This room should look familiar. Make your way to the center stairwell.

You should now be in the room with the two statues. Before you return the orb, prepare your characters for battle. This is it!

Once you return the orb to its final resting place, you will face Ramue and Shutat. Shutat will spout a bunch of gibberish about suffering. He will ask you to join him. *Just say no!*

Ramue is the weaker of the two, so go after her first. She has 1,200 Vitality Points and some powerful spells at her disposal, but her physical attacks are weak. Check the Monster Compendium (Appendix) for specifics. Shutat has 1,500 Vitality Points and better armor. His spells are also a bit tougher, so don't waste any time. Finish him off as soon as you can!

Once Ramue and Shutat are defeated, you will face Akkadias! He looks like a constipated alien from a recent science fiction movie named after a certain summer holiday. His most dangerous attack is his Soul Blast. It does approximately 20 to 30 Vitality Points of damage per blast. Expect to get hit by it twice per round. He is *very difficult* to fight! He has 4,200 Vitality Points, so unload everything you have on him. Good luck!

Once he is defeated, you must face his twin brother. Just kidding! Sit back, relax, and enjoy the ending!

CHAPTER SIX

✠ ITEMS INDEX

The following are the various items you'll stumble across in your adventures, along with a list of the weapons and armor carried by each character. The prices of those items available for purchase are included, along with a brief description of those items available to everyone. Some items cannot be bought in stores, but all items have a resale value of 75 percent of their value.

Note: Numbers in parentheses indicate the price of an item.

* Designates a cursed item.

COMMON ITEMS

Ancient Tablet: A magic scroll that allows you to raise the Ocean Pyramid when all four of its sections are collected and used in their corresponding temples.

Angel's Ocarina: (2,000) Restores Vitality Points to the entire party.

Antidote: (20) Cures poison and paralysis afflictions.

Awaken Stone: (1,150) Works like an Awaken Spell.

Blizzard Card: (1,000) Works like an Ice Spell.

Blizzard Scroll: (3,000) Works like an Ice Spell against all enemies.

Confusion Feather: (1,300) Works like a Confusion Spell.

Counter Orb: (1,000) Enhances the chance to perform a Counter Attack.

Critical Jewel: (1,000) Enhances the chance to perform a Critical Attack.

Cure Herb: (200) Cures poison and paralysis afflictions.

Dragon Card: (2,000) Works like a Steiner Spell.

Flame Card: (1,000) Works as a Fire Spell.

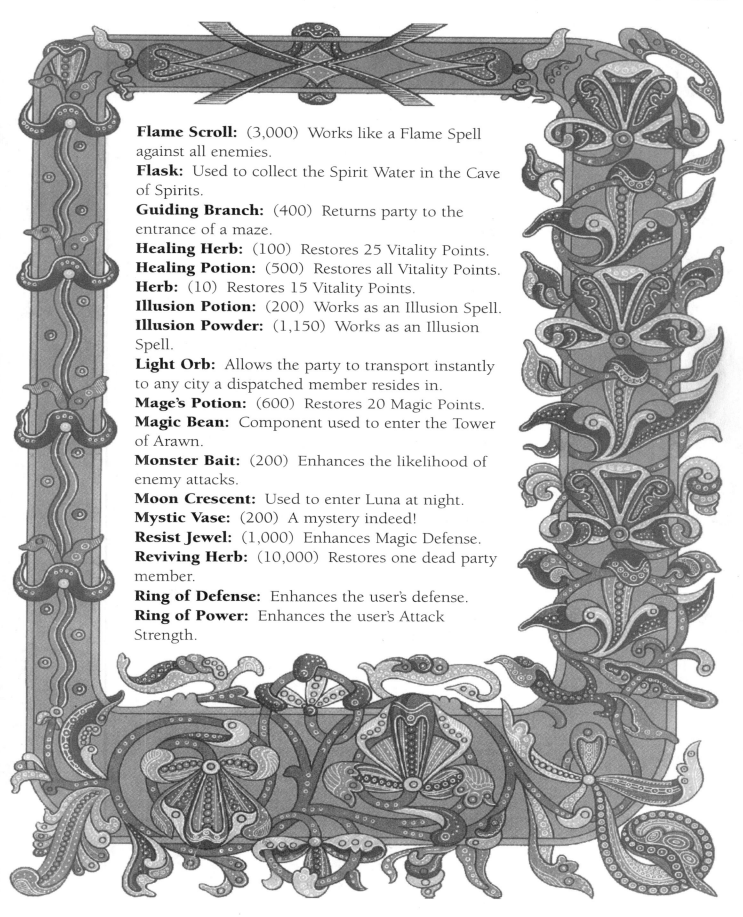

Flame Scroll: (3,000) Works like a Flame Spell against all enemies.

Flask: Used to collect the Spirit Water in the Cave of Spirits.

Guiding Branch: (400) Returns party to the entrance of a maze.

Healing Herb: (100) Restores 25 Vitality Points.

Healing Potion: (500) Restores all Vitality Points.

Herb: (10) Restores 15 Vitality Points.

Illusion Potion: (200) Works as an Illusion Spell.

Illusion Powder: (1,150) Works as an Illusion Spell.

Light Orb: Allows the party to transport instantly to any city a dispatched member resides in.

Mage's Potion: (600) Restores 20 Magic Points.

Magic Bean: Component used to enter the Tower of Arawn.

Monster Bait: (200) Enhances the likelihood of enemy attacks.

Moon Crescent: Used to enter Luna at night.

Mystic Vase: (200) A mystery indeed!

Resist Jewel: (1,000) Enhances Magic Defense.

Reviving Herb: (10,000) Restores one dead party member.

Ring of Defense: Enhances the user's defense.

Ring of Power: Enhances the user's Attack Strength.

*Ring of Revenge: Cursed item.

Seraphic Ring: (10,000) Enhances the user's defense.

Silence Crystal: (1,050) Works like a Silence Spell.

Skeleton Key: Allows you to open any locked door or treasure chest.

Slow Card: (1,200) Works as a Slow Spell.

Smoke Bomb: (500) Enhances the party's chance to run from battle.

Source of Agility: Raises the user's speed.

Source of Courage: Raises the user's level by one.

Source of Defense: Raises the user's defense.

Source of Growth: Raises the user's Experience Points.

Source of Magic: Raises the user's Magic Points.

Source of Power: Raises the user's attack strength.

Source of Wisdom: Raises the user's intelligence.

Statue of Gaea: Used to open the walkway to and from Gaea Island.

Tempest Jewel: (1,000) Enhances the chances for a Double Attack.

Thunder Card: (2,000) Works like a Thunder Spell.

Thunder Vase: (20,000) Works like a Thunder Spell against all opponents.

Tornado Card: (1,000) Works like a Wind Spell.

Unicorn Horn: Cures afflictions of all party members.

Vase of Life: Used to collect Nature's Water and to enter the Tower of Arawn.

Vision Crystal: (300) Allows a greater field of vision to the party on the Map Screen.

Wind Vase: (15,000) Works like a Wind Spell against all opponents.

World Map: Allows users to study their relative positions on Earth.

CHARACTER'S ITEMS

FINN'S ITEMS

WEAPONS

Short Sword - 100
Middle Sword - 280
Long Sword - 490
Broad Sword - 850
Great Sword - 1,500
Tempest Sword - 2,200
Rune Sword - 3,000
Guardian Blade - 7,000
Mystic Blade - 8,500
Counter Blade - 10,000
Mithril Blade - 12,000
Dragon Blade

ARMOR

Light Shield -70
Wood Shield - 110
Steel Shield - 230
Spike Shield - 370
Battle Shield - 620
Mithril Shield - 760
*Chaos Shield - 910
Cloth Jerkin - 80
Leather Plate -140
Bronze Plate - 240
Iron Plate - 430
Steel Plate - 750
Silver Plate - 1,300
Dragon Scale - 2,300
Mithril Scale - 4,000

SAMSON'S ITEMS

WEAPONS

Middle Axe - 120
Steel Axe - 300
Broad Axe - 520
Tomahawk - 870
Battle Axe - 1,600

War Axe - 2,300
Tempest Axe - 3,200
Rune Axe - 5,300
Earth Breaker - 9,000

ARMOR

Leather Bracer - 60
Gauntlet - 100
Rune Gauntlet - 460
Mazin Gauntlet - 590
Warrior's Gauntlet - 640
Mithril Gauntlet - 720
*Demon's Gauntlet - 900
Bronze Mail - 110
Steel Mail - 320
Chain Mail - 590
Heavy Mail - 1,150
Great Mail - 2,000
Mystic Mail - 3,800
Mithril Armor - 6,500
Evil Armor - 11,000

TONT'S ITEMS

WEAPONS

Wooden Rod - 80
Short Rod - 250
Bronze Rod - 450
Iron Rod - 830
Steel Rod - 1,350
Lunar Rod - 1,780
Shield Rod - 2,300
War Rod - 3,200
Tempest Rod - 6,200
Stun Rod - 6,200
Drain Rod
Defense Wand - 8,300
Malicious Rod - 14,000

ARMOR

Cloth Hood - 50
Leather Hood - 100
Magical Hood - 100
Travel Hood - 210
War Hood - 300

Wizard's Hood - 420
Summoner Hat - 680
*Death Hood - 800
Cloth Garment - 90
Travel Garment - 150
Leather Garment - 260
Magic Cape - 400
Wind Cloak - 720
Wizard's Cloak - 1,000
Mystic Cloak - 2,000
Cloak of Light - 3,800

ANNIE'S ITEMS

WEAPONS

Wooden Rod - 80
Short Rod - 250
Bronze Rod - 450
Iron Rod - 830
Steel Rod - 1,350
Lunar Rod - 1,780
Shield Rod - 2,300
War Rod - 3,200
Priest's Cane - 4,800
Tempest Rod - 6,200
Stun Rod - 6,200
Drain Rod - NA
Malicious Rod - 14,000

ARMOR

Ribbon - 40
Silk Ribbon - 90
Holy Ribbon - 160
Angel Ribbon - 250
Goddess Ribbon - 340
Athena Ribbon - 480
Floral Dress - 70
Travel Dress - 120
Journey Dress - 220
Battle Dress - 380
Tempest Dress - 700
Fairy Dress - 970
Seraphic Robe - 1,600
*Robe of Darkness - 9,500

EDWARD'S ITEMS

WEAPONS

Wooden Rod - 80
Short Rod - 250
Bronze Rod - 450
Iron Rod - 830
Steel Rod - 1,350
Lunar Rod - 1,780
Shield Rod - 2,300
War Rod - 3,200
Mage's Staff - 4,500
Elder's Wand - 4,600
Tempest Rod - 6,200
Stun Rod - 6,200
Drain Rod - NA
Magic Staff - NA
Malicious Rod - 14,000

ARMOR

Cloth Hood - 50
Leather Hood - 100
Magical Hood - 100
Travel Hood - 210
War Hood - 300
Wizard's Hood - 420
Sage's Hood - 610
Gundalf Hood - 700
*Death Hood - 800
Cloth Garment - 90
Travel Garment - 150
Leather Garment - 260
Magic Cape - 400
Wind Cloak - 720
Wizard's Cloak - 1,000
Mystic Cloak - 2,000
Cloak of Light - 3,800

LORELE'S ITEMS

WEAPONS

Power Knuckles - 6,600
Mystic Knuckles - 9,500

ARMOR

Silk Scarf - 470
Power Scarf - 730
Battle Gi - 3,000
Dragon Gi - 5,400

DOMINO'S ITEMS

WEAPONS

Darts - 2,500
Short Knife - 3,300
Throwing Knife - 4,900
Mithril Dagger - 6,800
Mystic Dagger - 9,000

ARMOR

Bandanna - 320
Sailor Bandanna - 450
Oath Bandanna - 880
Soft Leather - 1,800
Hard Leather - 3,100
Strong Leather - 5,700
Captain's Leather - 11,000

appendix
✤ monster compendium

Monster	V.P.	Strategy	Special Attacks and Abilities	Comments
Akkadias	4200	Survive	Soul Blast Summon 4; Heal	He's the ruler of the underworld for a reason. He is as dangerous as he is ugly. Hit him with everything you have left. Good Luck… You'll need it!
Amazon	18	Blades	Sword Charge	Amazons are excellent with their swords, and can heal with herbs.
Amazon Priestess	24	Fire; Ice	Confuse; Herbs	Stronger than your average Amazon, and they have the power to confuse your party.
Armor, Dead	48	Fire; Ice; Illusion;	Void	Dead Armor is haunted plate mail. It was created to withstand sword blows, so use your magic.
Living Armor	38	Ice; Thunder	Sleep	Living Armor is a formidable opponent. It is armor, so your blades will not do a great deal of damage. Stick with Ice and Thunder Magic.
Armor, Phantom	50	Ice; Illusion;	Void	Phantom Armor is also haunted plate mail. Try to use magic.
Assassin	30	Ice	Multiple Attacks	Assassins rely on their stealth, speed, and razor sharp daggers in battle. Fortunately for you, they don't wear heavy armor.
Bandore Commander	500	Void and other Strong Magic Spells	Attack Spell; Multiple Attacks; Heal	Bandore Commanders are the best fighters in the Bandore Army. Treat them like Boss Characters.
Bandore Soldier	45	Void and other Strong Magic Spells	Attack Spell; Multiple Attacks; Heal	Bandore Soldiers are pretty tough. There is no questions why their army is feared.
Barrog	104	Ice; Thunder; Most Powerful Magic	Paralyze Party; Thunder 2; Fire Breath 3	Barrogs are the toughest of demons. They attack twice per round with powerful magical attacks. Take them out quickly, or you'll be in for a really long day!
Basilisk	52	Fire	Paralysis	Don't let their silly appearance fool you.
Bat	12	Blades; Fire	Sleep	Bats are only dangerous in the beginning of the game, but if they are paired with a stronger enemy, their Sleep spell could be the end of you.
Bat, Sand Cave	60	Blades; Fire	Sleep; Calls for Help	Bats found in the Sand Cave are quite dangerous especially in numbers.
Bat, Small	7	Blades	–	Killing Small Bats is a great way to build Experience in the beginning of the game.
Bat, Vampire	47	Blades	Wild Stare (Sleep)	These bats will put you to sleep, and move in for the kill.
Black Aerial	65	Blades; Fire; Ice	Sleep; Wind 2	Black Aerials are extremely dangerous in groups. Their Wind Spells wound everyone in your party.
Black Knight	300	Powerful Spells	Fire; Thunder	You encounter the Black Knight at the end of the Sand Cave. If your party is in good health, you shouldn't have a problem.
Blood Pudding	22	Fire	Calls other Blood Puddings.	Blood Puddings are disgusting. Be thankful that you can't smell them. You can defeat them with blades, but Fire works much better.
Bug Bear	32	Fire	–	Bug Bears are found in forests, and are very strong. Lucky for you that their fur coats are flammable.
Burial	56	Ice	Fire Breath	Burials have fairly strong attacks, and a powerful breath of fire.
Cockratice	30	Fire	Halting Stare	Cockratice's can stop you in your tracks with their Halting Stare. Probably because your party members are laughing them.
Dagoot	1300	Hit him with everything you have!!!	Silence 2; Wind 3	Here is your chance to avenge Steiner! Use your magic before he silences your party. You may also want to carry Healing Potions because Annie may lose her abilities to cast Healing Spells.
Dark Priest	22	Blades	Heal 2	Just a Fat Man in a Cheap Robe.
Dark Bishop	40	Blades	Healing Rain	Another Fat Man, but Bishops hit harder and their Healing Rain can heal several members of their party.
Demon	79	Ice; Thunder; Blades	Help; Wind 3	Their thick skin protects them against your blades, and forget about using Fire - Remember where these guys live!
Demon, Greater	91	Blades; Ice; Holy Light	Paralysis; Thunder	Greater Demons: Need we say more?

Monster	V.P.	Strategy	Special Attacks and Abilities	Comments
Demon Hornet	13	Blades; Fire	Paralysis	You'll encounter Demon Hornets in the beginning of the game. Blades work fine, but if you want to defeat them in a hurry, use Fire.
Demon, Razor	46	Blades; Strong Magic	Calls for Help; Thunder 1; Sleep	Razor Demons have good armor against blades, so be careful.
Demon, Water	900	Fire	Ice; Heal	FIRE FIRE FIRE!!!
Demon's Pet	64	Thunder	Poison	These Pets are tougher than your average guard dog. They have great defenses against blades, and have strong physical attacks.
Devil Insect	78	Fire	Illusion; Paralysis	Devil Insects have good armor against blades, but weak defenses against magic.
Dire Wolf	27	Blades	Calls for Help	A single Dire Wolf can be dispatched with blades, but will call for help when endangered.
Dragon, Green	70	Fire; Ice	Poison	Green Dragons are very rare. Use magic to defeat them quickly.
Dragon, Ice	72	Fire; Titan	Blizzard Breath	Ice Dragons are found in the Ice Caves. Fire works very well.
Dragon, Mirage	66	Ice; Thunder	Illusion 2	Mirage Dragons have good defenses against blades. They will also cast Illusion Spells on your party. Magic is the best way to smite this menace.
Dragon, Red	88	Ice; Silence; Undhine	Fire Breath 2	Red Dragons are feared in all realms. Their scales offer them protection from physical attacks, and their great strength allows them to crush party members. Ice Magic works well against them.
Dragon, Shadow	105	Undhine	Fire Breath	Shadow Dragons are the strongest of Dragons. Lucky for you they are only found in the Underworld.
Dragon, Young	63	Ice	–	Young Dragons have good Armor and strong attacks, but seldom use any Magic.
Ekidona	59	Ice; Undhine	Poison; Thunder	Repeated encounters with Ekidonas will greatly weaken your party. Their poison is lethal, and their Thunder Spells will take their toll.
Ekidona, Elder	67	Ice; Undhine	Poison; Thunder	Unfortunately for you, Elder Ekidonas are stronger than their younger kin.
Elf	20	Ice	Wind 1; Illusion	These Elves take great joy in firing arrows at your characters hiding in the back row. Elves often carry Guiding Branches.
Elf, Dark	51	Ice	Wind Magic	Dark Elves are very accurate with their arrows. They have the ability to score Critical Hits. Use Ice Magic to defeat them quickly.
Elf, High	35	Blades; Holy Light	Wind 2	High Elves have good defenses against Magic. Your best bet is to charge with Cold Steel.
Evil Shaman	50	Blades; Ice	Herbs; Titan 1; Resurrection	Evil Shaman can bring their fallen comrades back to life at full health, but have weak defenses against blades.
Fenril	53	Blades	Scream	Fenril are found in the Ice Caves. They have many hit points, but do not do a great deal of damage. Save your magic for the tougher enemies.
Flying Mouse	15	Blades	–	Flying Mice are mere pests. Their agility makes them hard to hit, but they don't pose a great enough threat to warrant Powerful Magical Attacks.
Frog, Killer	11	Ice	Paralysis	The moist skin of the Killer Frog protects it from Fire, but makes it more susceptible to Ice Attacks.
Frog, Poison	14	Ice	Poison	Poison Frogs are more dangerous than their Killer cousins because of their ability to secrete a lethal toxin.
Gargoyle	33	Ice	Halting Stare	The stone skin of a Gargoyle protects it from Blades and Fire, but an Ice attack can cause their skin to turn brittle.
Gel, Huge	47	Fire; Ice	–	Huge Gel are more difficult to kill than their slimy cousins, but they are easily disposed of with magical attacks.
Ghost	25	Fire	Thunder 1; Ice 1	The Ghosts in this game definitely are not friendly. Their Ice and Thunder Spells can quickly make a bad day worse. Use Fire.
Ghoul	25	Fire	Paralysis	Ghouls prowl the graves at night in search for food. Their gruesome touch can paralyze a frightened party member, but their dry decayed skin burns very well.

Monster	V.P.	Strategy	Special Attacks and Abilities	Comments
Giant, Fire	50	Ice; Undhine	Fire 2	Fire Giants can take a great deal of punishment, and can ignite your party. Because they dwell near volcanoes, Ice works very well.
Giant, Ice	64	Fire	Ice 2	Ice Giants have the ability to freeze your party, but they are extremely susceptible to Fire Attacks.
Giant, Venom	53	Blades	Poison	Venom Giants can spit a deadly toxin on your party. Use blades to take them out quickly.
Glade	900	Attack Magic; Ice	Fire 2; Heal	Get ready for a long battle. Keep attacking, and using Annie's Healing Rain. Hit him hard!
Goblin	14	Ice	Herbs	Goblins are weak foes, but have the intelligence to use Herbs. Ice and blades work well.
Goblin, Giant	52	Blades	Herbs	Not to worry, Giant Goblins are a bit tougher than their smaller cousins, but pose no serious threat.
Golem, Clay	31	Ice; Undhine	–	Clay Golems are well protected against physical attacks, but magical attacks work very well.
Golem, Metal	60	Ice; Thunder; Most Powerful Spells	Confuse	Metal Golems are the best armored of the Golems, and they have the ability to Confuse your party members.
Golem, Stone	40	Ice; Titan	–	Stone Golems are well protected against physical attacks and hit very hard! Use Ice and Titan Magic.
Griffin	50	Blades; Ice	–	Griffins swoop down and attack. Lucky for you, they do not use magic.
Harpy	24	Fire	Illusion Powder; Calls for Help	Harpies can use Illusion Powder on your party which makes them difficult to hit with physical attacks. Luckily their feathers burn very well.
Hell Hound	41	Ice	Fire Breath	Hell Hounds can breathe fire, but are extremely vulnerable to Ice Attacks.
Harpy, Siren	37	Fire; Ice	Poison; Wind 2; Confusion	Siren Harpies are much more dangerous than your average Harpy. They can attack your entire party with Magic and Poison. Their armor provides a strong defense against blades.
Hippogriff	57	Fire	–	Hippogriffs have strong attacks and good defenses against physical attacks. They sometimes carry jewels.
Hobgoblin	21	Ice	–	Goblins are all alike. WEAK!
Hydra	48	Ice	Multiple Attacks and Counterattacks	Because of the Hydra's many heads, they can attack several times per round, and often counterattack when attacked.
Hydra, Pyro	52	Ice	Multiple Attacks and Counterattacks	Pyro-Hydras are very similar to Hydras, but fire based.
Hydra Warrior	95	Fire	Multiple Attacks; Thunder 2	Hydra Warriors are incredibly strong. They may cast up to two Thunder 2 spells per round. Ignite them as soon as you can!
Ice Warrior	26	Fire	Sleep; Herbs; Ice	Ice Warriors are tough if you fight them hand to hand. A little fire goes a long way.
Illusionist	36	Blades	Illusion	Illusionists have good defenses against magic, but weak armor against physical attacks.
Imp	39	Ice	Confuse; Calls for Help	Never expect a fair fight. Imps also know when to retreat.
Killer Bee	9	Blades	Poison	The attacks of the Killer Bees are weak, but they have the ability to poison. Kill them fast if you are low on antidotes.
Kobold	11	Blades	Retreating	Kobolds are especially good at deserting their allies and running like sissies.
Lich	55	Silence	Void	Liches are undead wizards. They have good defenses against fire, and superhuman physical attacks. Their most dangerous attack is a Void spell, which can instantly kill several of your party members. If you are attacked by a group, kill the Liches as fast as you can!!!
Kobold Lord	16	Blades	Herbs	Kobold Lord basically means lord of the wimps. Crush them.
Lizard Man	23	Ice	War Amulet	Lizard Men carry War Amulets which raise the physical attributes of their allies. If they get too strong, Ice them.
Lizard Warrior	31	Ice	–	Lizard Warriors are exactly like Lizard Men, only stronger.

Monster	V.P.	Strategy	Special Attacks and Abilities	Comments
Manticore	59	Blades; Ice; Most Powerful Spells	Poison	Manticore have thick hides and strong jaws. They can also poison a party member. A combination of physical attacks and Ice Magic is your best bet.
Manticore Elder	64	Blades; Ice; Most Powerful Spells	Paralysis	Far from elderly, Manticore Elders are stronger, but will not poison your party members. Instead, they will paralyze your party members for several rounds in combat.
Mantrap	16	Fire	Sleeping Fog	Mantraps can put party members to sleep and attack them. They are plants, so they burn very well.
Minotaur Lord	56	Attack Spells combined with Blade Attacks	Dragon Roar Raises Attack Power	Minotaur Lords hit very hard, and have strong defenses against physical attacks.
Mold	11	Blades	–	It's just Mold!
Mystic Fungus	48	Fire	Explosion	Mystic Fungus can endure quite a bit of physical attacks. They can combust and damage a party member. Their physical attacks are extremely weak. You can easily defeat them with blades, but if you are in a hurry, use Fire.
Naga	36	Ice	Ice 2	Naga have incredibly strong physical attacks, and can spray your party with Ice. In this case, fight Ice with Ice.
Necromancer	74	Silence	Titan; Fire Drake; Heal; Void	Kill Necromancers as soon as you see them. They have very powerful spells, including Void, but are very susceptible to blade attacks.
Nightmare Queen	95	Fire; Ice; Holy Light	Ice 3; Resurrect	Nightmare Queens have good defenses against blades, so use Fire. They can bring their comrades back to life, so if they are paired with strong enemies, it may be wise to take the Nightmare Queens out first.
Ogre	45	Ice	–	Ogres use brute force. They can also endure quite a bit of physical punishment. However, they are susceptible to Ice Magic.
Ork	16	Ice	Herbs	Orks are a prime example of brute force. They hit hard and can defend against physical attacks very well. You can put them away quickly with Ice Magic.
Ork, High	19	Ice	Calls for Help; Herbs	High Orks are a bit tougher, and they can call in reinforcements.
Ork, Lord	26	Ice	Calls for Help; Herbs	Ork Lords are the strongest Orks that you will encounter. Luckily they have the same weaknesses as the lesser Orks.
Poltergeist	55	Blades; Ice	Paralysis	Poltergeists have strong physical attacks. Take them out quickly with Ice.
Raise	38	Fire; Ice	Thunder; Defense	Raises are much tougher than Ghosts. They have a good balance of Offensive and Defensive Magic. They have good defenses against Physical Attacks, but are susceptible to Magic Attacks.
Ramue	1200	Persistance	Firedrake 1; Titan 1; Multiple Attacks per Round	She cast spells relentlessly. On a positive note, her physical attacks are weak. Here is your chance for revenge!
Roper	22	Fire	Poison Spray	Ropers are dangerous because they can spray Poison on your party. They are members of the Plant Kingdom so Fire does a great deal of damage.
Royal Guard	93	Thunder; Titan	–	Royal Guards are the guardians of the Underworld. Their attacks are powerful, and their armor is enchanted.
Scorpion, Devil	18	Ice	–	Devil Scorpions are the strongest of the Scorpion family. Because they are cold blooded, Ice Magic does the most damage.
Scorpion, Giant	12	Blades	–	Giant Scorpions have thick armor, but it is only a matter of time before your blades can hack through.
Shutat	1500	Tenacity– Keep Fighting!	Undhine 1; Firedrake 2; Silence 2; Multiple Attacks per Round	Shutat is more powerful than Ramue. He has better armor, and his spells are more powerful. Hit him with everything you've got!

Monster	V.P.	Strategy	Special Attacks and Abilities	Comments
Skeleton	15	Fire	War Amulet	Skeletons are tougher than they look. They fight well and can use War Amulets on their allies to increase their fighting abilities. They defend against blades, but Fire will destroy them.
Skeleton Warrior	23	Fire	Paralysis	Skeleton Warriors are great fighters, and their touch can Paralyze a party member. Fire works very well against them.
Slime	6	Blades	–	Slime is on the bottom of the food chain for a reason.
Slime, Green	13	Fire	Poison	Green Slime is twice as strong as normal Slime, and it can Poison you. Because Slime has no armor, and no way to control its body temperature, Fire works very well.
Snow Bear	68	Fire	Paralysis	Snow Bears can cause Paralysis, but because they are used to cold climates Fire works well.
Snow Wolf	60	Fire	Ice 2	Snow Wolves have strong physical attacks, and can spray Ice all over your party. Fire works well on anything that lives in the snow and has fur.
Spinning Tail	13	Fire	–	Spinning Tails are carnivorous rabbits. Crush them.
Succubus	52	Ice; Holy Light; Blades	Ice 2	Male party members tend to get distracted by the bouncing movement of the Succubus. Don't hesitate, these female demons will destroy you.
Summoner	24	Blades	Summons Enemies; Fire 2; Herbs	Summoners have quite a bit of weapons at their disposal, but they have weak defenses against blades.
Summoner, Evil	43	Blades; Silence	Thunder 1; Heal 2; Sleep; Summon 3	Evil Summoners will tear you apart if you give them a chance, so DON'T. Silence them or rush in with Physical Attacks.
Sylph	28	Silence; Ice	Wind 1; Wind 2	Sylphs' Wind Magic is very powerful and harms your entire party. The longer this fight lasts, the more damage your party will take.
Thief	16	Blades	Knife Throw; Herbs	A Thief's speed enables them to perform multiple attacks per round.
Tumble Rabbit	9	Blades	–	A Tumble Rabbit is an overgrown rabbit. Don't waste your magic.
Undead Knight	70	Fire; Ice; Titan; Blades	Attack 2	Undead Knights are the toughest of the Undead soldiers. Their cold blood allows them to resist Ice, but they may be cleansed by Fire.
Undead Lector	81	Blades; Strongest Magic	Heal Rain 3; Holy Light 3; Illusion	Undead Lectors are very tough fat men in cheap robes. Unlike their predecessors, they have offensive magic that can harm your entire party.
Warlock	17	Blades; Silence	Fire 1; Fire 2; Herbs	Warlocks have weak armor and feeble attacks. They do have powerful spells at their disposal, but a few blade attacks will finish them.
Water Leaper	35	Ice	Paralysis	Water Leapers are the toughest of the frog family. They have the ability to charge and Paralyze you. Put these frogs on Ice.
Wight	51	Fire	Paralysis	Wights are basically powerful undead freaks. Fire can send them back to their graves.
Worm	19	Ice	Poison Spit	Worms rise up from the ground and attack with their large jaws and venom. You can use blades or Ice.
Worm, Vampire	45	Blades; Ice	Poison	Vampire Worms are much more difficult to defeat than their subterranean cousins. If you must resort to magic, use Ice.
Wyvern	50	Ice; Titan; Thunder	Poison	Wyverns are similar to dragons, but not as powerful. They can Poison you, but are susceptible to powerful spells.
Yeon	1150	Attack Spell; Strongest Spells	Thunder 3; Confusion 2	Use powerful spells that hit all 3 enemies in the beginning so you can take out his cronies in the first round. Then concentrate all of your firepower on Yeon.
Yeti	40	Fire	Ice 2	Yeti can attack your party with a blast of Ice. Counterattack with Fire magic.
Yeti Child	38	Fire	Ice	Just a lesser version of the Yeti.
Zombie	17	Fire	Poison	Zombies of this land are surprisingly acrobatic. They are poisonous, so defeat them quickly with Fire.

COMPUTER GAME BOOKS

1942: The Pacific Air War–The Official Strategy Guide	$19.95
The 11th Hour: The Official Strategy Guide	$19.95
The 7th Guest: The Official Strategy Guide	$19.95
Aces Over Europe: The Official Strategy Guide	$19.95
Across the Rhine: The Official Strategy Guide	$19.95
Alone in the Dark 3: The Official Strategy Guide	$19.95
Armored Fist: The Official Strategy Guide	$19.95
Ascendancy: The Official Strategy Guide	$19.95
Buried in Time: The Journeyman Project 2–The Official Strategy Guide	$19.95
CD-ROM Games Secrets, Volume 1	$19.99
CD-ROM Games Secrets, Volume 2	$19.99
CD-ROM Classics	$19.95
Caesar II: The Official Strategy Guide	$19.95
Celtic Tales: Balor of the Evil Eye–The Official Strategy Guide	$19.95
Cyberia: The Official Strategy Guide	$19.99
Cyberia²: The Official Strategy Guide	$19.95
Dark Seed II: The Official Strategy Guide	$19.95
Descent: The Official Strategy Guide	$19.99
Descent II: The Official Strategy Guide	$19.95
DOOM Battlebook	$19.95
DOOM II: The Official Strategy Guide	$19.95
Dragon Lore: The Official Strategy Guide	$19.95
Dungeon Master II: The Legend of Skullkeep–The Official Strategy Guide	$19.95
Fleet Defender: The Official Strategy Guide	$19.95
Frankenstein: Through the Eyes of the Monster–The Official Strategy Guide	$19.95
Front Page Sports Football Pro '95: The Official Playbook	$19.95
Fury³: The Official Strategy Guide	$19.95
Hell: A Cyberpunk Thriller–The Official Strategy Guide	$19.95
Heretic: The Official Strategy Guide	$19.95
I Have No Mouth, and I Must Scream: The Official Strategy Guide	$19.95
In The 1st Degree: The Official Strategy Guide	$14.95
Kingdom: The Far Reaches–The Official Strategy Guide	$19.95
King's Quest VII: The Unauthorized Strategy Guide	$19.95
The Legend of Kyrandia: The Official Strategy Guide	$19.95
Lords of Midnight: The Official Strategy Guide	$12.95
Machiavelli the Prince: Official Secrets & Solutions	$19.95
Marathon: The Official Strategy Guide	$19.95
Master of Orion: The Official Strategy Guide	$19.95
Master of Magic: The Official Strategy Guide	$19.95
MechWarrior 2: The Official Strategy Guide	$12.95
Microsoft Arcade: The Official Strategy Guide	$19.95
Microsoft Flight Simulator 5.1: The Official Strategy Guide	$19.95
Microsoft Golf: The Official Strategy Guide	$19.95
Microsoft Space Simulator: The Official Strategy Guide	
Might and Magic Compendium:	
The Authorized Strategy Guide for Games I, II, III, and IV	$19.95
Mission Critical: The Official Strategy Guide	$19.95
Myst: The Official Strategy Guide	$19.95
Online Games: In-Depth Strategies and Secrets	$19.95
Oregon Trail II: The Official Strategy Guide	$19.95
Panzer General: The Official Strategy Guide	$19.95
Perfect General II: The Official Strategy Guide	$19.95
Prince of Persia: The Official Strategy Guide	$19.95
Prisoner of Ice: The Official Strategy Guide	$19.95
The Residents: Bad Day on the Midway–The Official Strategy Guide	$19.95
Return to Zork Adventurer's Guide	$14.95
Ripper: The Official Strategy Guide	$19.99

Romance of the Three Kingdoms IV: Wall of Fire–The Official Strategy Guide	$19.95
Shannara: The Official Strategy Guide	$19.95
Sid Meier's Civilization, or Rome on 640K a Day	$19.95
Sid Meier's Civilization II: The Official Strategy Guide	$19.99
Sid Meier's Colonization: The Official Strategy Guide	$19.95
SimCity 2000: Power, Politics, and Planning	$19.95
SimEarth: The Official Strategy Guide	$19.95
SimFarm Almanac: The Official Guide to SimFarm	$19.95
SimLife: The Official Strategy Guide	$19.95
SimTower: The Official Strategy Guide	$19.95
Stonekeep: The Official Strategy Guide	$19.95
SubWar 2050: The Official Strategy Guide	$19.95
Terry Pratchett's Discworld: The Official Strategy Guide	$19.95
Thunderscape: The Official Strategy Guide	$19.95
TIE Fighter Collector's CD-ROM: The Official Strategy Guide	$19.99
Under a Killing Moon: The Official Strategy Guide	$19.95
WarCraft: Orcs & Humans Official Secrets & Solutions	$ 9.95
WarCraft II: Tides of Darkness–The Official Strategy Guide	$19.99
Warlords II Deluxe: The Official Strategy Guide	$19.95
Werewolf Vs. Commanche: The Official Strategy Guide	$19.95
Wing Commander I, II, and III: The Ultimate Strategy Guide	$19.95
X-COM Terror From The Deep: The Official Strategy Guide	$19.95
X-COM UFO Defense: The Official Strategy Guide	$19.95
X-Wing Collector's CD-ROM: The Official Strategy Guide	$19.95

VIDEO GAME BOOKS

3DO Game Guide	$16.95
Battle Arena Toshinden Game Secrets: The Unauthorized Edition	$12.95
Behind the Scenes at Sega: The Making of a Video Game	$14.95
Breath of Fire Authorized Game Secrets	$14.95
Breath of Fire II Authorized Game Secrets	$14.95
Complete Final Fantasy III Forbidden Game Secrets	$14.95
Donkey Kong Country Game Secrets the Unauthorized Edition	$ 9.95
Donkey Kong Country 2–Diddy's Kong Quest Unauthorized Game Secrets	$12.99
EA SPORTS Official Power Play Guide	$12.95
Earthworm Jim Official Game Secrets	$12.95
Earthworm Jim 2 Official Game Secrets	$14.95
GEX: The Official Power Play Guide	$14.95
Killer Instinct Game Secrets: The Unauthorized Edition	$9.95
Killer Instinct 2 Unauthorized Arcade Secrets	$12.99
The Legend of Zelda: A Link to the Past–Game Secrets	$12.95
Lord of the Rings Official Game Secrets	$12.95
Maximum Carnage Official Game Secrets	$ 9.95
Mortal Kombat II Official Power Play Guide	$ 9.95
Mortal Kombat 3 Official Arcade Secrets	$ 9.95
Mortal Kombat 3 Official Power Play Guide	$ 9.95
NBA JAM: The Official Power Play Guide	$12.95
Ogre Battle: The March of the Black Queen–The Official Power Play Guide	$14.95
Parent's Guide to Video Games	$12.95
PlayStation Game Secrets: The Unauthorized Edition, Vol. 1	$12.99
Secret of Evermore: Authorized Power Play Guide	$12.95
Secret of Mana Official Game Secrets	$14.95
Street Fighter Alpha–Warriors' Dreams Unauthorized Game Secrets	$12.99
Ultimate Mortal Kombat 3 Official Arcade Secrets	$ 9.99
Urban Strike Official Power Play Guide, with Desert Strike & Jungle Strike	$12.95

To Order Books

Please send me the following items:

Quantity	Title	Unit Price	Total
		$ _____	$ _____
		$ _____	$ _____
		$ _____	$ _____
		$ _____	$ _____
		$ _____	$ _____

Subtotal	$ _____
Deduct 10% when ordering 3-5 books	$ _____
7.25% Sales Tax (CA only)	$ _____
8.25% Sales Tax (TN only)	$ _____
5.0% Sales Tax (MD and IN only)	$ _____
Shipping and Handling*	$ _____
Total Order	$ _____

Shipping and Handling depend on Subtotal.

Subtotal	Shipping/Handling
$0.00–$14.99	$3.00
$15.00–$29.99	$4.00
$30.00–$49.99	$6.00
$50.00–$99.99	$10.00
$100.00–$199.99	$13.50
$200.00+	Call for Quote

Foreign and all Priority Request orders:
Call Order Entry department
for price quote at 916/632-4400

This chart represents the total retail price of books only
(before applicable discounts are taken).

By Telephone: With MC or Visa, call 800-632-8676, 916-632-4400. Mon-Fri, 8:30-4:30.
WWW {http://www.primapublishing.com}

Orders Placed Via Internet E-mail {sales@primapub.com}
By Mail: Just fill out the information below and send with your remittance to:

Prima Publishing
P.O. Box 1260BK
Rocklin, CA 95677

My name is _____

I live at _____

City _____ State _____ Zip _____

MC/Visa# _____ Exp. _____

Check/Money Order enclosed for $ _____ Payable to Prima Publishing

Daytime Telephone _____

Signature _____